The Tylos Period Burials
in Bahrain

The Tylos Period Burials in Bahrain, Volume 2,
The Hamad Town DS 3 and Shakhoura Cemeteries

Mustafa Ibrahim Salman and Søren Fredslund Andersen © 2009

ISBN 978 87 7934 512 6

Copyediting and revision: Helen Knox
Layout: Hanne Kolding
Cover: Hanne Kolding
Drawings: Søren Fredslund Andersen, Karsten Mikkelsen and Ali Omran
Photographs: Søren Fredslund Andersen and Bahrain National Museum
Printed by: Narayana Press

Published by:
Culture & National Heritage
Kingdom of Bahrain
in association with
Moesgård Museum and
Aarhus University

Distributed by
Aarhus University Press
Langelandsgade 177
DK-8200 Aarhus N
Denmark
www.unipress.dk

Gazelle Book Services Ltd.
White Cross Mills,
Hightown
Lancaster,
LA1 4XS
www.gazellebooks.co.uk

The David Brown Book Company (DBBC)
P.O. Box 511
Oakville CT 06779
USA
www.oxbowbooks.com

The Tylos Period Burials in Bahrain

VOLUME 2

The Hamad Town DS 3 and Shakhoura Cemeteries

by Mustafa Ibrahim Salman and Søren Fredslund Andersen

with contributions by
Khaleel Al Faraj, Naseem Haider, Mohammad Hassan, Abdul Kareem Jassem, Judith Littleton,
Abbas Ahmed Salman, Abdul Rahman Sobah and Dawod Yusuf

Kingdom of Bahrain مملكة البحرين

وزارة الثقافة و الإعلام
Ministry of Culture & Information

Acknowledgements

Mustafa Ibrahim Salman

This book is the result of twenty years of excavations conducted by the Directorate of Archaeology and Heritage in the burial mounds of Hamad Town area DS3 and Shakhoura.

I would like to acknowledge my indebtedness to all those who made this research possible. My thanks to Her Excellency Shaikha Mai Bint Mohamed Bin Ibrahim Al-Khalifa, Assistant Undersecretary of Culture and National Heritage for her encouragement and assistance in making our thoughts real. I also gratefully acknowledge the continued assistance of Dr Flemming Højlund from Moesgård Museum. Special thanks to my colleague Dr Søren Fredslund Andersen from University of Aarhus who supervised this research and supplemented the work done by Bahraini archaeologists. I also appreciate the invaluable help of Mr Khalid Al-Sindi, Head of the Archaeology Department.

In particular, I would like to thank the following: Ali Omran (draftsman), Saleh Ali (photographer), Isa A'Raheem (acting head of the collections Department), Maryem Al-Haermy (head of the excavation report archive) and Mohammed Saleh, together with archaeologists and other staff in the Bahrain National Museum, for their continued help and effort.

Table of contents

Introduction

Only two cultural periods in Bahrain had a burial tradition with individual tombs covered with a tumulus. In the Bronze Age large tumuli fields were built during the so-called Dilmun period. In this period, Bahrain became a centre within a north-east Arabian kingdom, which was heavily involved in maritime trade and especially the copper trade between Oman and the Mesopotamian urban centres (Højlund 2007). In the 1950s a second group of burials in tumuli was first described (Field 1951). This type of burial is now known to have been used from *c.* 200 BC and probably until the coming of Islam in the seventh century AD, and thus during most of the so-called Tylos period (Andersen 2007). The Tylos period tombs and the ones from the Bronze Age are easy to distinguish, because the Tylos period tombs were most often built of stones set in mortar and plastered, whereas the Bronze Age tombs comparable in size to the Tylos period tombs were built with drystone walls. Furthermore, the Tylos period tombs do not have alcoves, which is a common feature in the Bronze Age.

In Volume 1 (Andersen 2007) the glass vessels and tableware pottery found in the Tylos period burials were presented and discussed. A priority was to create an independent chronological system, to enable the burials to be placed in a broader cultural and historical context. Five distinctive phases were described and dated mainly by the imported glass vessels to the period from *c.* 200 BC until *c.* AD 700 (Table 1).

Phase	Dating
I	200–50 BC
II	50 BC–AD 50
III	AD 50–150
IV	AD 150–450
V	AD 450–700

Table 1. The chronological phases for the Tylos period burials defined in Volume 1.

The findings from the later part of the period (i.e. Phases IV and V) indicate that glass vessels were only placed in the tombs during certain periods, possibly in the fourth century AD and again in the sixth/seventh century. Glass vessels dating to the intermediate period (fifth to sixth century AD) are absent and the continuation of pottery types between the periods is limited. However, since the glass is imported and most of the other grave goods do not possess precise dating information, the hiatus is most likely to be in the import of foreign goods rather than in the discontinuity of burials.

The stylistic analyses of the glass and pottery vessels also shed some light on the cultural and historical development of Bahrain in the Tylos period. The most significant result was the identification of a significant increase in the quantity of grave goods in the relatively short Phase III. This was likely to be the result of benefits from the international trade between the Roman Empire and India in the first century AD, in which the people of Bahrain seem to have taken an active part. In this period the glass vessels were mainly imported from production centres in the eastern Mediterranean region and the local Gulf pottery was highly influenced by contemporary prototypes used in the Roman Empire. This development seems to have started in Phase II. In Phase IV the trade routes or the organization of the trade may have changed, leaving only a minor profit in Bahrain. Hereafter the glass was mainly imported to Bahrain from Mesopotamian or Iranian production centres.

It is the aim of this volume to provide the reader with a broader impression of cemeteries, tombs and grave goods from the Tylos period by presenting the excavations of a selection of mounds, rather than focusing on the most spectacular findings or specific find groups.

The cemeteries
A selection of eleven mounds with 244 tombs from the Hamad Town area is presented in Chapter 2 and eighteen mounds with 563 tombs from Shakhoura in Chapter 3 (Figure 1). These excavations have been conducted by the staff of the Bahrain National Museum as salvage operations to clear land for modern development.

The selected excavations from Hamad Town were conducted in the 1985–1986 season in the DS3 Area (Figure 2). These excavations were selected because the skeletal remains were studied, thus providing significant additional information.[1]

The mounds in Hamad Town were relatively low, most of them being only *c.* 1 m high and positioned closely together. In six of the mounds, Bronze Age tombs were found and to the east of the Tylos period cemetery a larger group of Bronze Age mounds could also be observed (Figure 3).

The cemetery north-west of Shakhoura village has been significantly diminished over the last twenty-five years, but a group of mounds from the Tylos period was still preserved in 2007. A similar area north-west of Saar village was completely excavated ten to twenty years ago (Figure 1) and the group of mounds in Shakhoura is now the only remnant of the mound fields from the Tylos period (Figure 4). The largest mounds so far excavated in Bahrain were also in the Shakhoura area, both regarding size and number of tombs. Mound 1-1992-93, with its 188 tombs was until recently the one with most tombs, but recent excavations at Mound B2 have revealed more than 300 tombs (Figure 5).[2] The area has produced some spectacular finds from the Tylos period in Bahrain (Lombard 1999) and was therefore selected for further analysis to see whether these finds were indicative of the stratification of Tylos society or whether they were merely the result of minor chronological and regional differences.

[1] The skeletal remains were studied by Dr Judith Littleton (1998) and additional information has generously been made available for this study (cf. Appendix 2).

[2] The excavations have been named in rather descriptive terms as follows: 1) Area, named after the nearest village; 2) Mound number; and 3) Excavation season. An example is Shakhoura, Mound 1, Season 1992–1993, which in the following will be abbreviated to Shakhoura, Mound 1-92-93. The combination of mound number and season is important, since a mound called number 1 etc. exists in more than one area, but two mounds with the same number in the same area were not likely to have been excavated in the same season (although this cannot be completely excluded either). When a tomb was encountered, it was normally numbered in sequence, so a reference to a specific tomb will be for instance, "Shakhoura, Mound 1-92-93, Tomb 17". For further details see Volume 1: 13–15.

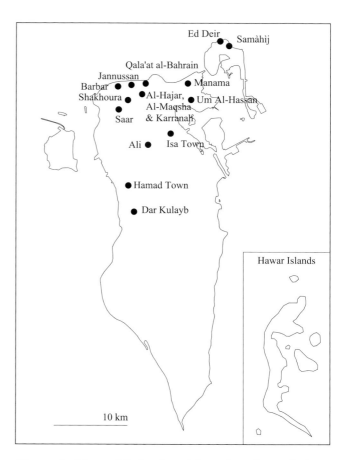

Figure 1. Map of Bahrain with archaeological sites of the Tylos period.

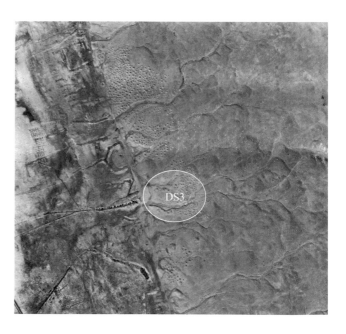

Figure 2. Aerial photo of Hamad Town with the DS3 Area marked.

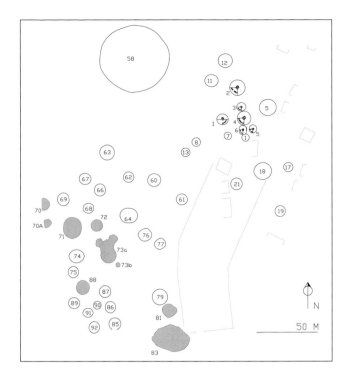

Figure 3. Sketch map of part of the DS3 area. Mounds presented in Chapter 2 are marked in grey, whereas the other mounds are from the Bronze Age. Modern constructions are in grey line.

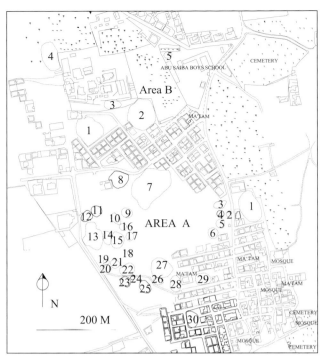

Figure 5. Sketch map of the Shakhoura cemetery made by the Bahrain National Museum in 1996.

Figure 4. Aerial photograph taken in 1977 of the Shakhoura cemetery. Identified mounds are marked with the mound number and excavation season.

The presentations of the excavations in Hamad Town and Shakhoura in Chapters 2 and 3 are based on the records made by the supervisors of the excavations. They usually recorded the dimensions of the tombs and whether it was built in a cutting in the bedrock, directly on the bedrock, or in the mound fill.

The finds

The contents of the tombs were also noted during excavation, but a consistent terminology was not available, which makes the categories used in this presentation rather broad. Some finds have been identified in the Bahrain National Museum storerooms and in these cases the inventory number has been recorded. For the glass and pottery vessels identified in the storeroom, the catalogue number assigned in Volume 1 has also been recorded. However, museum storage based on the find context has not been attempted and only a relatively limited number of finds from each excavation have been positively identified during this study. It has therefore not been possible to reclassify the material. In the following, the different categories for finds used in Chapters 2 and 3 are described.

9

Figure 8. Lath-turned ivory containers with stoppers from Shakhoura, Mound A1-1996-97, Tombs 14 and 97.

Figure 10. Silver ring with letters in an unknown script from Hamad Town, Mound 73-1985-86, Tomb 55.

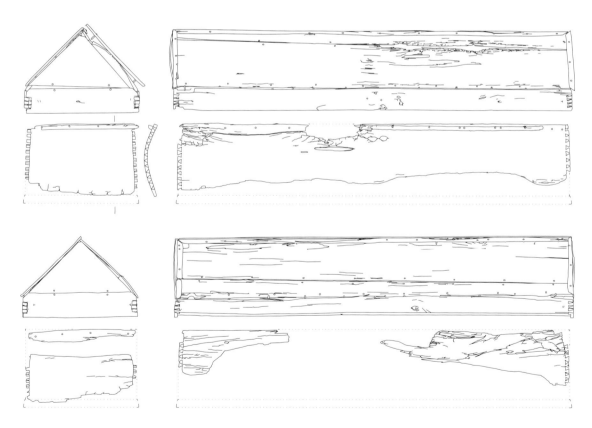

Figure 9. Wooden coffin made of Pakistani rosewood from Shakhoura, Mound A1-1996-97, Tomb 44.

1 m

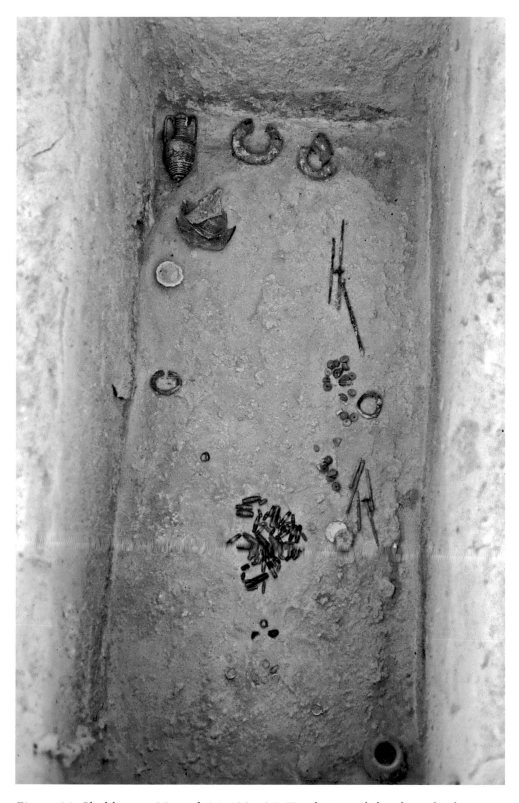

Figure 11. Shakhoura, Mound A1-1996-97, Tomb 47 with beads and other grave goods in situ.

Figure 12. Ivory or bone objects similar in shape to spindle whorls, but probably used as beads from Shakhoura, Mound A1-1996-97, Tomb 47.

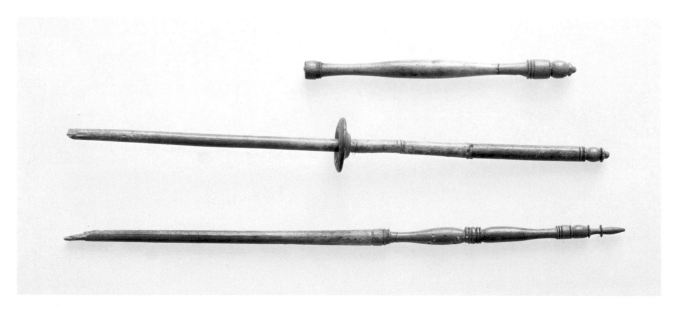

Figure 13. Relatively well-preserved dress pins made of ivory. From Hamad Town, but the full context information is lost.

Figure 14. Plaster figurines from Shakhoura, Mound 1-1994-95, Tomb 2.

Figure 16. Clay figurine from Saar, Mound 2-1992, Tomb 57.

Figure 15. Clay figurine from Shakhoura, Mound A1-1996-97, Tomb 65.

Figure 17. Bone figurine from Shakhoura, Mound A1-1996-97, Tomb 47.

Figure 18. Bronze bells from Shakhoura, Mound A1-1996-97, Tomb 97.

The Hamad Town Area, The DS 3 Cemetery

2

Edited by Mustafa Ibrahim Salman

Mound 30, 1985-86
Naseem Haider

Mound 30 was situated in the centre of a new building complex. The mound measured *c*. 30 x 30 m and had a height of 2.58 m above the surrounding terrain. It was round in shape, but was damaged on all sides by vehicles. The top of the mound was uneven. The southern half of the mound was flat and higher than the northern half. A few large stones were visible on top of the mound towards the centre. On the northern slope of the mound there was a pit close to the top of the mound. The eastern slope was not very steep and to the north, it was damaged close to the top. On the southern slope, there were shallow pits on the upper side of the slope. Sand and small stones covered the mound.

The excavation of the mound was laid out in six trenches each measuring 9.50 x 14.50 m and baulks were left between the trenches. The filling of the mound consisted of sandy rubble. Fragments of human bones, pottery sherds of different wares, beads of semi-precious stones, pieces of bronze objects, seashells and charcoal were found in the mound fill. Below the mound was a layer of brown sand with pebbles. The mound was completely excavated. A plastered platform was exposed 0.74 m above Tomb 26. It covered an area of 2.04 x 1.64 m and the thickness of the grey gypsum plaster varied from 2–6 cm.

In all, forty-six tombs were found in Mound 30. Of them forty-one were of the Tylos type and five could be dated to the Dilmun period. Most of the Tylos tombs were dug into the soil below the original surface on which the mound was built, at depths varying from 0.1 to 0.62 m. Some of these tombs were built directly on the bedrock and only nine chambers (nos 18, 22, 23, 23-A, 24, 27, 28, 29 and 30) were built at different levels in the mound fill above the original surface. The thickness of the chamber walls ranged from 0.12 to 1.17 m. The tombs were orientated in all directions and no system of placing the skeletons in the tomb in a specific direction could be identified.

Figure 19. Mound 30 before excavation.

Type	No.	BNM No.	Cat. no.	Material	Find type	Number	Remark
Tomb	1			Stone	Bead		
Tomb	1			Stone	Bead	23	
Tomb	2			Bronze	Ring	1	
Tomb	2			Stone	Bead	61	
Tomb	2			N/A	Bead	1	
Tomb	7			Stone	Bead	1	
Tomb	8			Stone	Bead	14	
Tomb	9			Sea shell	N/A[5]	1	
Tomb	10			Pottery	Fragments		
Tomb	12			Pottery	Pot		Fragments.
Tomb	13			Bronze	Fragments		
Tomb	13			Stone	Bead	4	
Tomb	13			Bronze	Fragments		
Tomb	14			Wood	Coffin		Fragments.
Tomb	17			Pottery	Jar	1	
Tomb	18			Pottery	Bowl	1	
Tomb	18			Bronze	Necklace	2	
Tomb	18			Stone	Bead	67	
Tomb	19			Organic material	Reed mat		Fragments.
Tomb	20			Wood	Coffin		Fragments.
Tomb	20			Ivory	Pin head	2	
Tomb	20			Stone	Bead	1	
Tomb	21	832-2-88	J.3	Glazed pottery	Jar	1	
Tomb	21			Organic material	Burned textile		Fragments.
Tomb	21	808-2-88	BV.22	Glazed pottery	Jar	1	
Tomb	21			Glazed pottery	Cup	1	
Tomb	21			Ivory	Pin head	1	
Tomb	21			Bronze	Nail	3	
Tomb	21			Bronze	Fragments		
Tomb	21			Stone	Bead	1	
Tomb	21			Bronze	Finger ring	1	
Tomb	22			Organic material	Reed mat		Fragments.
Tomb	25			Glazed pottery	Bowl		
Tomb	28			Seashell	N/A		
Tomb	31			Wood	Coffin		Fragments.
Tomb	31			Bronze	Ring	1	
Tomb	31			Bronze	Bangle	1	
Tomb	31			Ivory	Button	5	
Tomb	31			Bronze	Nail	1	
Tomb	31			Stone	Bead		Many.
Tomb	31			Stone	Bead	58	
Tomb	31			Bronze	Fragments		
Tomb	34			Stone	Bead	1	
Tomb	34			Ivory	Pin head		Many.
Tomb	34			Ivory	N/A	1	
Tomb	39	10202-2-91	CZ.2	Glazed pottery	Bottle	1	
Tomb	39			Glazed pottery	Bottle	1	
Tomb	39			Sea shell	N/A	2	
Tomb	39			Bronze	Pin	1	
Tomb	40	7236-2-91	BE.72	Glazed pottery	Sherd		
Tomb	40			Stone	Bead	3	
Tomb	40			Stone	Bead	82	
Tomb	40			Pottery	Sherd	3	
Tomb	41	373	BL.18	Glazed pottery	Jar	1	
Tomb	41	342	CX.6	Glazed pottery	Bowl	1	Found outside tomb.

Table 4. List of finds (DS3 cemetery, Mound 30).

[5] N/A = not available (abbreviation used when the information is lacking).

Figure 21. Section of Mound 30.

Figure 22. Mound 30, Tomb 5 with two skeletons – one pushed aside.

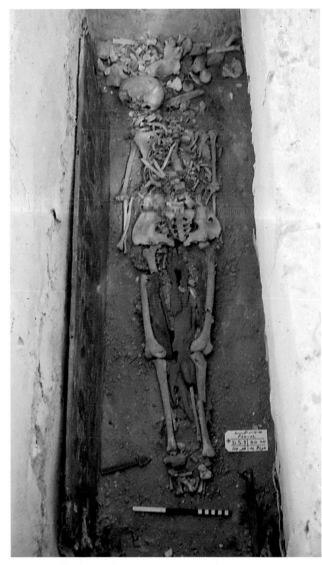

Figure 23. Mound 30, Tomb 14 with remains of a wooden coffin and skeletons.

Figure 24. Mound 30, Tomb 15 with capstones in situ.

Figure 25. Mound 30, Tomb 17 with a skeleton of a child and jar in the corner.

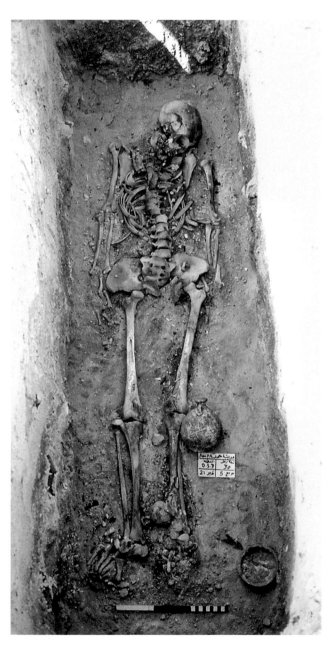

Figure 26. Mound 30, Tomb 21 with skeleton and grave goods.

Figure 27. Mound 30, Tomb 22 with a skeleton with the arms crossed over the chest.

Figure 29. Mound 30, Burial jar 7 with opening sealed with mortar.

Figure 30. Mound 30, Jar found outside a tomb in Trench 5.

Figure 28. Mound 30, Tomb 41 where the lower part of the skeleton can be seen with two glazed pottery vessels.

Mound 70, 1985-86

Abbas Ahmad Salman

To the north of Mound 70 was bare land, to the south lay Mound 70A and a garden and to the east lay Mound 73 at a distance of 15 m.

Mound 70 was round in shape and measured *c.* 10 to 11.5 m in diameter. It had a height of 1.15 m above the surrounding terrain. A few large and small stones were visible on the surface of the mound at the centre. The rest of the mound was covered with small stones.

The excavation of the mound was carried out in four quadrants. Quadrant 1 was in the north-western section, Quadrant 2 in the south-west, Quadrant 3 in the south-east, and Quadrant 4 in the north-east. No baulk was left between the trenches and the eastern half was excavated first. The mound was completely excavated.

The filling of the mound consisted of brown sand and many small stones. Below the mound was a layer of brown sand with pebbles mixed with seashell as well as some pieces of pottery sherds. In total four tombs were found, three of them of the Tylos type and one from the Dilmun period. Tomb 1 was in the centre of the mound and Tombs 2 and 3 were in Quadrant 4. The Dilmun tomb was in the northern part of the mound and initially labelled Tomb 5. No grave goods from the Tylos period tombs were recorded.

Figure 31. Mound 70 before excavation.

Type	No	Trench	Built	Disturbed	Length	Width	Depth	Remarks
Tomb	1		On bedrock	Yes	195	65	95	
Tomb	2		On bedrock	Yes	205	50	81	
Tomb	3		On bedrock	Yes	100	48	60	
Tomb	4		On bedrock	Yes	135	65	68	Dilmun type

Table 5. List of tombs (DS3 cemetery, Mound 70).

Type	No.	BNM No.	Cat. no.	Material	Find type		Remark
Tomb	4			Pottery	Fragments		Dilmun period

Table 6. List of finds (DS3 cemetery, Mound 70).

24

Figure 32. Mound 70 after excavation. Initially the stone pile seen to the left was believed to be a tomb.

Figure 33. Section of Mound 70.

Figure 34. Reused tomb, Mound 70, Tomb 2.

Figure 35. Mound 70, Tomb 4. Dilmun period tomb.

Mound 70A, 1985-86

Mohammad Hassan

To the north of this mound lay Mound 70 at a distance of 4 m and to the east lay Mound 71 at a distance of 4 m. To the west was a garden and south of Mound 70A was bare land. The development of Hamad Town required the removal of only half of Mound 70A to clear land for a water pipeline. On top of the mound, a fence ran in a north–south direction and only the part of the mound lying to the east of the fence was excavated.

The mound was excavated in twelve trenches measuring 6 x 4 m and orientated east–west. A 1 m-wide baulk was left between the excavated areas, but removed during the final part of the excavation to uncover tombs underneath. The surface of the mound was covered with small stones and the mound fill consisted of sand with small stones. The exact numbers of tombs and burial jars were not noted.

Figure 36. Mound 70A before excavation.

Figure 37. Mound 70A after excavation.

Type	No	Trench	Built	Disturbed	Length	Width	Depth	Remarks
Tomb	1	6	On bedrock	Yes	200	60	80	
Tomb	2	1-2	On bedrock	Yes	190	65	80	
Tomb	3	2	On bedrock	Yes	190	59	75	Empty.
Tomb	4	2	On bedrock	Yes	198	62	90	
Tomb	5	5	On bedrock	Yes	260	60	70	
Tomb	6	2	On bedrock	Yes	200	60	80	
Tomb	7	3	Above bedrock	Yes	70	55	62	
Tomb	8	3	On bedrock	Yes	210	60	90	
Tomb	9	3	On bedrock	Yes	180	55	85	
Tomb	10	3	On bedrock	Yes	176	40	60	
Tomb	11	5	On bedrock	Yes	175	48	82	Documentation incomplete.
Tomb	12	5			200	50	88	
Tomb	13	6	On bedrock	Yes	197	54	60	
Tomb	14	6			220	55	90	
Tomb	15		N/A	N/A	N/A	N/A	N/A	Tomb not emptied during excavation.
Tomb	16		N/A	N/A	N/A	N/A	N/A	Tomb not emptied during excavation.
Tomb	17	6	On bedrock	Yes	116	50	64	
Tomb	18	8	On bedrock		215	70	90	
Tomb	19	8	On bedrock		200	70	80	
Tomb	20			N/A	N/A	N/A	N/A	Tomb not emptied during excavation.
Tomb	21	8	On bedrock	Yes	245	60	95	
Tomb	22		N/A	N/A	N/A	N/A	N/A	Tomb not emptied during excavation.
Tomb	23		N/A	N/A	N/A	N/A	N/A	Tomb not emptied during excavation.
Tomb	24	8	On bedrock		270	170	40	
Tomb	25	7	On bedrock	Yes	193	46	65	
Tomb	26	7	On bedrock	Yes	185	45	50	
Tomb	27	7	On bedrock		184	50	55	

Table 7. List of tombs (DS3 cemetery, Mound 70A).

Type	No.	BNM No.	Cat. no.	Material	Find type	Number	Remark
Tomb	1	2262-2-90	18.1	Glass	Bottle	1	
Tomb	1			Ivory	Pin head	2	
Tomb	1			Seashell	N/A		Many.
Tomb	1			Bronze	Fragments		
Tomb	1	A13440		Silver	Finger ring	1	
Tomb	1			Stone	Bead		Many.
Tomb	1			Bronze	Spindle	1	
Tomb	1	2638-2-90	CC.2	Pottery	Little jug	1	
Tomb	2			Stone	Bead		Many.
Tomb	2			Seashell	N/A		Many.
Tomb	2			Ivory	Pin head	1	
Tomb	6	355	CN.9	Pottery	Jug	1	
Tomb	6	A6117	CL.5	Pottery	Jug	1	
Tomb	6			Iron	Fragments	1	
Tomb	7			Pottery	Fragments	1	
Tomb	8			Bronze	Spindle	1	
Tomb	8			Iron	Fragments	1	
Tomb	12			Glazed pottery	Bowl	1	
Tomb	12			Pottery	Jar	1	
Tomb	12			Pottery	Cup	1	
Tomb	12			Iron	Fragments		
Tomb	12			Pottery	Jar	1	
Tomb	17	A15424		Stone & glass	Bead		Many.
Tomb	17	A12294		Bronze	Pin	1	Fragments.
Tomb	17	A15424		Glass	Bead		Many.
Tomb	18			Pottery	Fragments		
Tomb	19			Bronze	Ring	1	
Tomb	21	A5644	BO.23	Glazed pottery	Pot	1	
Tomb	21			Pottery	Jar	1	
Tomb	24			Pottery	Fragments		
Tomb	24			Pottery	Jar	1	
Tomb	24			Pottery	Jar	1	
Tomb	24			Iron	Fragments	1	
Fill	Sq. 6	A12941		Stone & glass	Bead		Many.

Table 8. List of finds (DS3 cemetery, Mound 70A).

Figure 38. Section of Mound 70A.

Figure 39. Mound 70A, Tomb 1 with skeletons and grave goods.

Figure 40. Mound 70A, Tomb 6 after excavation.

Figure 41. Mound 70A, Tomb 11 after excavation.

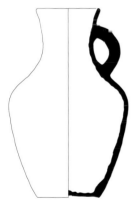

Figure 42. Type CN hard-fired ware jug from Mound 70A-1985-86, Tomb 6.

Figure 43. Grave goods in Mound 70A, Tomb 17.

Figure 44. Capstones of Mound 70A, Tombs 17 and 18.

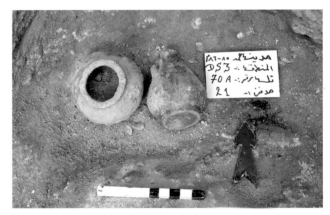

Figure 45. Grave goods in Mound 70A, Tomb 21.

Figure 46. Mound 70A, Burial jar 2 in situ.

Figure 47. Mound 70A, Burial jar 3 after excavation.

31

Mound 71, 1985-86

Mohammad Hassan

To the north of Mound 71 lay Mound 69 and Mound 68 at distances of 5 and 6 m respectively. To the west lay Mound 70A at a distance of 9 m, to the south lay Mound 74 at a distance of 8 m and towards the east Mounds 73 and 72 lay very close.

Mound 71 was round in shape, but the southern side was damaged. It measured 14 to 18 m across and had a height of 1.5 m above the surrounding terrain. The southern half of the mound was higher than the northern half and the mound was covered with small stones.

The excavation of the mound was carried out in four quadrants. Quadrant 1 was in the north-western section, Quadrant 2 in the south-west, Quadrant 3 in the south-east and Quadrant 4 in the north-east. No baulk was left between the trenches and the eastern half was excavated first. The mound was completely excavated.

Nineteen tombs were discovered, together with one burial jar found in Quadrant 4 with another pottery vessel. Around Tomb 3 in the western part of the mound there were some stones, which could be the remains of a wall or more likely the remains of stone packing, used to keep the sides of the mound in place. Tombs 16 and 17 were double-chambered, which seems to be a late development in tomb architecture (see Chapter 4).

Figure 48. Mound 71 before excavation.

Type	No.	Trench	Built	Disturbed	Length	Width	Depth	Remarks
Tomb	1		On bedrock	Yes	185	53	65	
Tomb	2		On bedrock	Yes	182	42	63	
Tomb	3		Above bedrock	Yes	203	68	110	
Tomb	4		Above bedrock	Yes	116	45	43	
Tomb	5		On bedrock		195	45	65	Bone pushed aside.
Tomb	6		On bedrock		125	47	45	
Tomb	7		On bedrock		187	48	55	
Tomb	8		On bedrock	Yes	170	50	35	Empty.
Tomb	9		On bedrock	Yes	185	56	54	
Tomb	10		On bedrock		185	42	50	
Tomb	11		On bedrock	Yes	187	50	62	
Tomb	12		On bedrock	Yes	190	50	70	
Tomb	13		On bedrock	Yes	180	60	72	
Tomb	14		On bedrock	Yes	180	50	60	
Tomb	15		Into bedrock	Yes	195	50	50	
Tomb	16		On bedrock	Yes	283	83	93	Empty.
Tomb	17		On bedrock	Yes	290	80	93	Empty.
Tomb	18		On bedrock	Yes	55	40	45	Empty.
Tomb	19		On bedrock	Yes	190	50	43	Empty.

Table 9. List of tombs (DS3 cemetery, Mound 71).

Type	No.	BNM No.	Cat. no.	Material	Find type	Number	Remark
Tomb	3			Glazed pottery	Bowl	1	Fragments.
Tomb	4	A13382		Bronze	Bracelet	1	
Tomb	4			Bronze	N/A		Many.
Tomb	4	A14284		Stone & glass	Bead	14	
Tomb	4	A14284		Glass	Bead		Many.
Tomb	4	7287-2-91	CC.15	Pottery	Jar	1	
Tomb	7			Glass	Bottle	1	
Tomb	7			Ivory	Dress pin head	2	
Tomb	9			Pottery	Jar	1	
Tomb	9			Glass	Bottle	1	
Tomb	9			N/A	Ring	1	With gem.
Tomb	15			Pottery	Fragments		
Tomb	15			Seashell	N/A	1	
Tomb	15	A14863		Bronze	Bead	3	

Table 10. List of finds (DS3 cemetery, Mound 71).

Figure 49. Mound 71 after excavation.

Figure 50. Section of Mound 71.

Figure 51. Mound 71, Tomb 4 after excavation.

Figure 52. Cover of Mound 71, Tomb 6.

Figure 53. Mound 71, Tomb. 9 after excavation.

Figure 54. Mound 71, Tombs 16 and 17 after excavation. An example of a double-chambered tomb, which seems to be a late development.

Figure 55. Mound 71, Burial jar 1 before excavation.

Mound 72, 1985-86
Mustafa Ibrahim Salman

To the north of Mound 72 lay Mound 68 at a distance of 2 m, to the west was Mound 71 at a distance of 7 m and to the south-east was Mound 73 at very close range.

Mound 72 was round in shape and measured 9.5 to 10 m in diameter. The surface of the mound was uneven, with a depression in the northern and south-eastern sections. In the southern section, there was a small hole. Small stones and soft sand covered the mound.

The excavation of the mound was conducted in four quadrants. Quadrant 1 was in the north-western section, Quadrant 2 in the south-west, Quadrant 3 in the south-east and Quadrant 4 in the north-east. No baulk was left between the trenches and the mound was completely excavated.

Two tombs from the Tylos period were found, together with one tomb from the Dilmun period. The Dilmun tomb had a ring wall around it, which at the time of excavation was in relatively poor condition, as stones had been robbed from it.

Figure 56. Mound 72 before excavation.

Figure 57. Mound 72 after excavation.

36

Figure 58. Section of Mound 72.

Figure 59. Mound 72, Tomb 3 after excavation.

Type	No	Trench	Built	Disturbed	Length	Width	Depth	Remarks
Tomb	1			Yes				Dilmun tomb. Destroyed.
Tomb	2		On bedrock	Yes	193	55	52	
Tomb	3		On bedrock	Yes	195	41	62	

Table 11. List of tombs (DS3 cemetery, Mound 72).

Type	No.	BNM No.	Cat. no.	Material	Find type	Number	Remark
Tomb	2			Stone	Bead		
Tomb	2			Bronze	Ring	1	

Table 12. List of finds (DS3 cemetery, Mound 72).

Mound 73, 1985-86

Mustafa Ibrahim Salman

Mound 73 was situated in the centre of the DS 3 mound complex. To the north of the mound lay Mound 72 at a distance of 6 m, to the west lay Mound 74 at a distance of 0.5 m, to the south lay Mound 87 at a distance of 14 m and to the east lay Mound 76 at a distance of 11 m.

It was a relatively big mound, which measured 32 to 34 m across. The top of the mound was uneven and there were three higher parts. The highest was in the south. A few stones were visible on the surface in the centre of the mound, but otherwise sand and small stones covered the mound. The slopes of the mound were damaged.

The mound was divided into eight squares of 10 x 11 m each and baulks were left between the squares. The excavations started in the western part and continued until the whole mound was excavated. Finally, all the baulks between the squares were removed.

The filling of the mound consisted of sand with small stones. Some tombs were used twice or more.

The orientation of tombs was different and the skeletons were placed in both directions in the burial chambers. In the centre of the mound was a house in which seven rooms were uncovered. The walls and floors of the house were built of stone and mortar, and the floors were plastered. In these rooms, four tombs of the Tylos type were built in different parts, reusing some of the walls.

Tomb 1 had no capstones and was presumably robbed in ancient times, but it appears to have been a tomb with many interments, and the grave goods indicate that many of them should be dated to Phase IV. Tomb 18 is a very interesting tomb, since it appears to have been built with a façade containing an entrance that could be reopened for further interments. Unfortunately none of the finds from Tomb 18 provide any dating evidence, but the position of the tomb on the edge of the mound and at a significantly higher level than the tomb (no. 48) in front of Tomb 18, indicates that Tomb 18 is a relatively late tomb built in Mound 73.

Figure 60. Mound 73 before excavation.

Type	No	Trench	Built	Disturbed	Length	Width	Depth	Remarks
Tomb	1	1	Above bedrock	Yes	189	69	94	
Tomb	2	2	Above bedrock	Yes	185	50	43	
Tomb	3	2	Above bedrock	Yes	175	40	55	
Tomb	4	2		Yes	193	46	61	
Tomb	5	2			185	55	63	
Tomb	6	2	Above bedrock	Yes	190		64	
Tomb	7	2	Above bedrock	Yes				
Tomb	8	2	Above bedrock	Yes	195	58	70	
Tomb	9	2	Above bedrock	Yes	192	60	58	
Tomb	10	2	Above bedrock		94	38	46	
Tomb	11	3	Above bedrock	Yes	192	53	45	
Tomb	12	3	Above bedrock		200	63	67	
Tomb	13	6	Above bedrock		190	50	75	
Tomb	14	7	Above bedrock	Yes	198	53	53	
Tomb	15	4	Into bedrock	Yes	183	38	51	
Tomb	16	4-5	Into bedrock	Yes	194	51	47	
Tomb	17	4	Into bedrock	Yes	104	49	40	
Tomb	18	7	Above bedrock	Yes	680	212	109	
Tomb	19	5	Above bedrock		190	58	30	
Tomb	20	5	Above bedrock	Yes	201	62	95	
Tomb	21	5	Above bedrock	Yes	186	62	56	
Tomb	22	4	Above bedrock	Yes	191	53	53	
Tomb	23	5	Above bedrock	Yes	190	45	65	
Tomb	24	5	Above bedrock	Yes	202	48	53	
Tomb	25	5	Above bedrock	Yes	215	41	55	
Tomb	26	5	Above bedrock	Yes				
Tomb	27	5	Above bedrock	Yes	143	55	38	
Tomb	28	8	Above bedrock		195	52	66	
Tomb	29	5	Above bedrock		197	57	74	
Tomb	30	5	On bedrock	Yes	195	60	90	
Tomb	31	5	Above bedrock	Yes	199	60	94	
Tomb	32	5	On bedrock	Yes	105	52	53	Empty.
Tomb	33	5	On bedrock	Yes	200	64	100	
Tomb	34	5	Above bedrock		205	62	70	
Tomb	35	6	On bedrock		213	64	98	
Tomb	36	6	On bedrock		204	61	95	
Tomb	37	6	On bedrock		216	53	110	
Tomb	38	6	On bedrock	Yes	209	66	91	
Tomb	39	6	On bedrock		193	55	48	
Tomb	40	6	Above bedrock	Yes	200	53	61	
Tomb	41	6	Above bedrock	Yes	202	49	68	
Tomb	42	6	On bedrock		185	44	56	
Tomb	43	6	Above bedrock		104	52	46	
Tomb	44	6	On bedrock	Yes	196	60	50	
Tomb	45	6	On bedrock	Yes	192	50	53	
Tomb	46	6	On bedrock	Yes	192	50	80	
Tomb	46A	6	On bedrock		137	51	55	
Tomb	47	7	Above bedrock	Yes	120	57	55	
Tomb	48	7	On bedrock		185	54	67	
Tomb	49	7	On bedrock		117	40	56	
Tomb	50	7	On bedrock		177	48	70	
Tomb	51	9	On bedrock		190	50	65	
Tomb	52	9	On bedrock		193	42	65	
Tomb	53	8	Above bedrock		105	45	39	
Tomb	54	8	Above bedrock	Yes	220	44	60	
Tomb	55	8-9	On bedrock		190	57	75	
Tomb	56	8		Yes	120	85		
Tomb	57	9	Above bedrock		214	53	54	
Tomb	58	8	On bedrock	Yes	200	46	50	
Tomb	59	9	On bedrock	Yes	153	50	62	
Tomb	60	9	On bedrock		232	63	67	
Tomb	61	9	Above bedrock	Yes	210	40	58	
Tomb	62	9						
Tomb	63	9	On bedrock	Yes	185	47	58	
Tomb	64	9	On bedrock	Yes	102	49	43	
Tomb	65		On bedrock					

Table 13. List of tombs (DS3 cemetery, Mound 73).

Type	No	Square	Length	Max. Ø	Rim Ø	Remarks
Jar	1	5	84	44	12	
Jar	2	5				Jar was damaged. The bones of a child scattered.
Jar	3	5	74	42	20	
Jar	4	9	67	43	25	
Jar	5	9	56	32	14	Jar was not emptied during excavation.
Jar	6	5				Jar was damaged.

Table 14. List of burials jars (DS3 cemetery, Mound 73).

Type	No.	BNM No.	Cat. no.	Material	Find type	Number	Remark
Tomb	1			Glazed pottery	Jug	1	
Tomb	1	A14392	41.5	Glass	Bowl	1	
Tomb	1	310	CO.4	Pottery	Jug	1	
Tomb	1			Glass	Bottle	1	Fragments.
Tomb	1	A9068	25.6	Glass	Bottle	1	
Tomb	1	A6083	CN.10	Pottery	Jug	1	
Tomb	1			Pottery	Jar	1	
Tomb	1	929-2-88	41.12	Glass	Bowl	1	
Tomb	1			Bronze	Spindle	1	
Tomb	1			Glass	N/A	1	
Tomb	1			Bronze	Earring	2	
Tomb	1			Seashell	N/A	1	
Tomb	1	311	CN.7	Pottery	Jug	1	
Tomb	1	1074	CN.3	Pottery	Jug	1	
Tomb	1			N/A	N/A	1	
Tomb	1			Iron	Fragments		
Tomb	1	N/A	34.27	Glass	Bottle	1	
Tomb	1	A8941	38.1	Glass	Bottle	1	
Tomb	1			Glass	N/A	1	
Tomb	1	88-2-747	CL.7	Pottery	Jug	1	
Tomb	1			Bitumen	N/A	1	
Tomb	1			Glass	Beaker	1	Fragments
Tomb	1			Seashell	N/A	3	
Tomb	1			Ivory	Pin head	1	
Tomb	1			Stone	N/A	1	
Tomb	1			Bronze	Coin	1	
Tomb	1			Steatite	N/A	1	
Tomb	1	A11259	33.1	Glass	Bottle	1	
Tomb	1	A14384	12.8	Glass	Bottle	1	
Tomb	1			Bronze	Spindle	1	
Tomb	1			Glazed pottery	Cup	1	
Tomb	1	A4807	AQ.150	Glazed pottery	Bowl	1	
Tomb	1	A12887		Bronze	Needle	1	
Tomb	1			Steatite	Pin head	1	
Tomb	4	A4814	AQ.147	Pottery	Hollow-based bowl	1	
Tomb	4			Pottery	N/A	1	
Tomb	5			Gold	Earring	2	

Type	No.	BNM No.	Cat. no.	Material	Find type	Number	Remark
Tomb	5			Alabaster	Bowl	1	Fragments, with cover.
Tomb	5			Glass	Bottle	1	
Tomb	5			Bronze	Bracelet	1	Fragments.
Tomb	5			Bronze	Bracelet	1	
Tomb	5	A13970		Sliver	Finger ring	2	
Tomb	5	A16352		Bronze	Finger ring	2	
Tomb	5	A15439		Stone & bronze	Bead		Many.
Tomb	5	A14045		Glass	Gem	1	
Tomb	5			Bronze	Spindle	1	
Tomb	5			Glass	Bottle		Fragments.
Tomb	5			Bronze	N/A	1	
Tomb	5			Wood	N/A	1	
Tomb	6			Pottery	Jar	1	Fragments.
Tomb	6	A14185		Glass	Bead	2	
Tomb	6	A14185		Bone	Bead	1	
Tomb	6	A14185		Pottery	Bead	1	
Tomb	6			Bronze	Coin	1	
Tomb	10	A14688		Glass & bone	Bead	16	
Tomb	10			Bronze	Bracelet	1	
Tomb	11			Ivory	Pendant	2	
Tomb	11			Bronze	Finger ring	1	
Tomb	11	A15430		Stone & glass	Bead	29	
Tomb	12			Glazed pottery	N/A	1	
Tomb	12	4363-2-91-2	NON.24	Glazed pottery	Jug	1	
Tomb	12			Glazed pottery	Bowl	1	
Tomb	12			Pottery	Bowl	1	Fragments.
Tomb	12	9914-2-91	CC.9	Pottery	Little jug	1	
Tomb	12			Pottery	Bowl	1	
Tomb	12	A12091		Bronze	Spatula	1	
Tomb	13			Ivory	Pin head	1	
Tomb	16			Pottery	Bowl	1	Fragments.
Tomb	18			Pottery	Fragments		
Tomb	18			Iron	Fragments		
Tomb	18	A10560		Stone & glass	Bead	118	
Tomb	18			Bronze	N/A	1	
Tomb	18	A12865		Steatite	Grindstone	1	
Tomb	18	A14684		Stone & glass	Bead	93	
Tomb	18			Bronze	Ring	2	
Tomb	18			Bronze	Fragments		
Tomb	18	A10565		Stone & glass	Bead	37	
Tomb	18	A15258		Stone & glass	Bead	6	
Tomb	19			Pottery	Bowl	1	Fragments.
Tomb	25			Pottery	Fragments		
Tomb	25			Seashell	N/A	8	
Tomb	26			Seashell	N/A	2	
Tomb	27	A15077	7.5	Glass	Bottle	1	
Tomb	27	4693-2-90-2	DG.3	Pottery	Bottle	1	
Tomb	27			Bronze	N/A	2	
Tomb	28	A4731	BL.38	Glazed pottery	Jar	1	
Tomb	28			Glazed pottery	Bowl	1	Fragments.

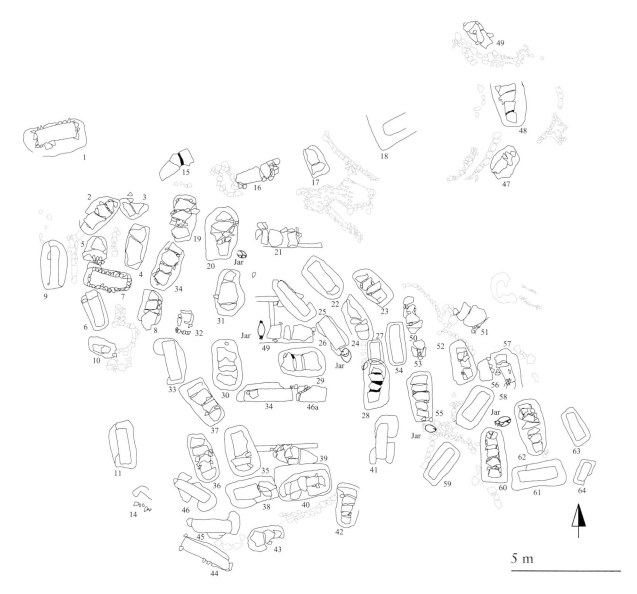

Figure 61. Plan of Mound 73 after excavation.

Figure 62. Mound 73 after excavation.

44

Figure 63. Tylos period tombs built into the remains of an earlier house reusing walls from the house.

Figure 64. Another view of the house, found in the centre of the mound.

Figure 65. Mound 73, Tomb 1 after excavation of the first layer of multiple interments.

Figure 67. Mound 73, Tomb 1 after excavation of the third layer.

Figure 66. Mound 73, Tomb 1 after excavation of the second layer.

Figure 68. Type 12 glass bottle from Mound 73-1985-86, Tomb 1.

Figure 69. Type 25 glass bottle from Mound 73-1985-86, Tomb 1.

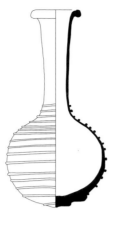

Figure 73. Type 41 glass bowl from Mound 73-1985-86, Tomb 1.

Figure 70. Type 33 glass bottle from Mound 73-1985-86, Tomb 1.

Figure 71. Type 33 glass bottle from Mound 73-1985-86, Tomb 1.

Figure 72. Type 38 glass bottle from Mound 73-1985-86, Tomb 1.

Figure 74. Type 41 glass bowl from Mound 73-1985-86, Tomb 1.

Figure 75. Two silver rings from Mound 73-1985-86, Tomb 5.

Figure 76. Mound 73, Tomb 14 after excavation.

Figure 77. Mound 73, Tomb 18 after excavation of the first layer of multiple interments.

Figure 78. Mound 73, Tomb 18 after excavation of the second layer.

Figure 80. Mound 73, Façade of Tomb 18.

Figure 79. View of Mound 73, Tomb 18 after excavation.

Figure 81. Type 7 glass bottle from Mound 73-1985-86, Tomb 27.

Figure 83. Mound 73, Tomb 35. Capstones before the tomb was opened.

Figure 82. Tombstone next to capstone of Mound 73, Tomb 30.

Figure 86. Type 32 glass
bottle from Mound
73-1985-86, Tomb 44.

Figure 87. Type 32 glass
bottle from Mound
73-1985-86, Tomb 44.

Figure 84. Incense burner and fragment of a plain
ware bottle of Type CC dating to Phase III from
Mound 73, Tomb 37.

Figure 85. Mound 73, Tomb 44 after excavation.

Figure 88. Type 41 glass bowl from Mound 73-1985-86, Tomb 44.

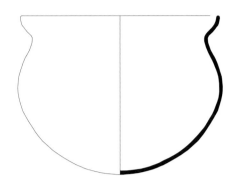

Figure 89. Type 41 glass bowl from Mound 73-1985-86, Tomb 44.

Figure 90. Type BY glazed ware bottle from Mound 73-1985-86, Tomb 51.

Figure 91. Finger ring made of silver from Mound 73-1985-86, Tomb 51.

Figure 92. Mound 73, Tomb 53 after excavation. The vessel in the north-east corner is made of alabaster.

Figure 93. Type 10 glass bottle from Mound 73-1985-86, Tomb 54.

Figure 94. Finger ring with inscription in an unknown script from Mound 73-1985-86, Tomb 55.

Figure 95. Type 11 glass bottle from Mound 73-1985-86, Tomb 60.

Figure 96. Mound 73, Burial jar 5 before excavation.

Mound 81, 1985-86

Mustafa Ibrahim Salman

Mound 81 was part of a cluster of mounds situated close together. To the west of Mound 81 was Mound 82 at a distance of 3 m, to the south was Mound 83 at a distance of 2.5 m, to the east was Mound 84 at a distance of 10 m and to the north-west laid Mound 79 at a distance of 5 m. To the north of Mound 81 lay Mound 77 at a distance of 42 m (See Figure 3).

Mound 81 was round in shape and measured 13.5 to 14 m in diameter and had a height of 1.27 m above the surrounding terrain. It was damaged by bulldozers on the northern side. It was flat on the top, although the northern half of the mound was slightly sunken. Small stones with soft sand covered the mound.

The excavation of the mound was laid out in four quadrants and no baulk was left between the excavation trenches. Quadrant 1 was in the north-western section, Quadrant 2 in the south-west, Quadrant 3 in the south-east and Quadrant 4 in the north-east. Quadrants 1 and 2 were excavated first, followed by Quadrants 3 and 4. The excavation revealed fifteen tombs. One tomb was situated in the centre of the mound with a ring wall around it, and it can be dated to the Dilmun period by its construction. The remaining fourteen tombs were of the Tylos type. Some of the Tylos tombs were built on top of the ring wall of the Dilmun tomb and others were built outside the ring wall. The filling of the mound consisted of mostly sandy rubble with small stones. The mound was completely excavated.

Figure 97. Mound 81 before excavation.

Figure 100. Mound 81 after excavation.

Figure 101. Section of Mound 81.

Figure 102. Mound 81, Tomb 1 with capstone sealed with mortar.

Figure 103. Detail of Mound 81, Tomb 1 which was disturbed in antiquity by tomb raiders or by reuse of the tomb.

Figure 104. A Type CC plain ware bottle in situ in Mound 81, Tomb 2.

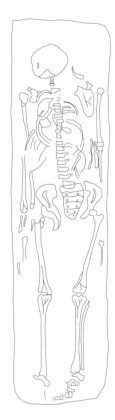

Figure 106. Mound 81, plan of Tomb 4 after excavation.

1 m

Figure 105. Mound 81, Tomb 4 before excavation.

Figure 107. Well-preserved skeleton from Mound 81, Tomb 4.

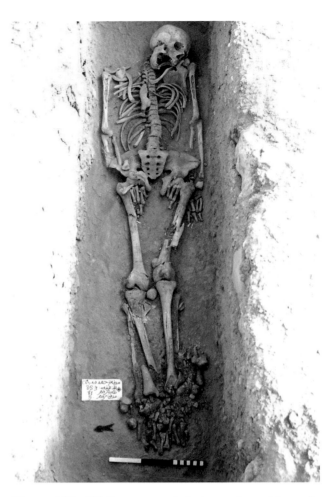

Figure 108. Well-preserved skeleton from Mound 81, Tomb 5.

Figure 109. Mound 81, Tomb 10. Dilmun type tomb.

Figure 110. Skeleton pushed aside in 12 in Mound 81.

1 m

Figure 111. Mound 81, plan of Tomb 12 after excavation.

Figure 112. Well-preserved skeleton from Mound 81, Tomb 13.

Mound 83, 1985-86

Mohammad Hassan

To the north of Mound 83 was Mound 81 situated at a very close distance. To the west lay Mound 85 at a distance of 14 m and to the east lay Mound 51 at a distance of 4 m. To the north-west lay Mound 82 also at a very close distance.

Mound 83 was a relatively big mound for the DS 3 area and measured 22 to 32 m across. It was rectangular and orientated north–south and had a maximum height of 1.95 m above the surrounding terrain. A bulldozer had cut into the eastern slope of the mound. The surface of the mound was uneven and two higher parts existed. One was in the west and created a relatively steep western slope and the other was slightly lower and situated in the southern part of the mound. The northern half of the mound was higher than the southern half. A few medium-sized stones were visible on the surface in the north-eastern part of the mound. The mound was covered with small stones.

Eight squares trenches were laid out for the excavation with 1 m-wide baulks between them. The excavation started in the western half of the mound in Trench 1 to 4 and continued in the eastern half (Trench 5 to 8). After all the trenches had been excavated, the baulks were removed. The mound fill consisted of brown sand and many small stones. The excavation revealed fifty-two tombs, all of them presumably dating to the Tylos period.

Figure 113. Mound 83 before excavation.

Type	No.	BNM No.	Cat. no.	Material	Find type	Number	Remark
Tomb	30			Stone	Bead		Many.
Tomb	31			Bitumen	Fragments	0	
Tomb	31	A4837	A.7	Pottery	Bowl	1	
Tomb	31	A4537	CQ.4	Pottery	Jar	1	
Tomb	31			Stone	Bead		Many.
Tomb	31			Ivory	Pin head	2	
Tomb	31			Bronze	Spindle	1	
Tomb	31			Pottery	Bowl	1	
Tomb	31			Bronze	Earring	1	Fragments.
Tomb	31			Bronze	Ring	1	Fragments.
Tomb	32			Bronze	Ring	1	Fragments.
Tomb	35			Glazed pottery	Jar	1	
Tomb	35			Ivory	Pin head	2	
Tomb	35			Bronze	Spindle	1	
Tomb	36			Pottery	Fragments		
Tomb	36			Seashell	N/A		Many.
Tomb	39			Pottery	Fragments		
Tomb	39			Stone	Bead	1	
Tomb	40			Stone	Bead		Many.
Tomb	40			Bronze	Ring	1	
Tomb	41			Pottery	Jar	1	Fragments.
Tomb	41			Bronze	Spindle	1	
Tomb	42	2551-2-90	BE.28	Pottery	Bowl	1	
Tomb	42	2244-2-90	BL.9	Glazed pottery	Jar	1	
Tomb	43	9960-2-91	CC.8	Pottery	Fragments		
Tomb	44	A8914	25.3	Glass	Bottle	1	
Tomb	44	A14390	30.1	Glass	Bottle	1	
Tomb	44			Bronze	Fragments		
Tomb	44	A14389	25.8	Glass	Bottle	1	
Tomb	44			Stone	Bead	1	
Tomb	44	A5649	DA.10	Pottery	Jar	1	
Tomb	44	91-2-7201	CQ.2	Pottery	Jar	1	
Tomb	44	198	CQ.1	Pottery	Jar	1	
Tomb	44	A4732	NON.18	Glazed pottery	Jar	1	
Tomb	44			Seashell	N/A	2	
Tomb	44			Ivory	Pin head	2	
Tomb	44			Pottery	Fragments		
Tomb	45			Stone	Bead		Many.
Tomb	49			Seashell	N/A	1	
Tomb	49			Stone	Bead	1	
Tomb	51			Ivory	Pin head	2	
Tomb	51			Seashell	N/A	1	
Jar	8	A9049	15.4	Glass	Bottle	1	
Jar	10			Stone	Bead		Many.
Jar	10			Bronze	Earring	1	

Table 20. List of finds (DS3 cemetery, Mound 83).

Figure 114. Part of Mound 83 excavated.

Figure 115. Mound 83 after excavation.

Figure 116. Plan of Mound 83 after excavation.

Figure 117. Mound 83, Tomb 8 with capstones before excavation.

Figure 118. Mound 83, Tomb 8 with remnants of a wooden coffin.

Figure 119. Mound 83, Tomb 16 where the skeletons from earlier burials were pushed aside to make room for the secondary interment.

Figure 120. Mound 83, Tomb 26 with skeleton in hocker position and Phase IV grave goods.

Figure 121. Mound 83, Tomb 31 after excavation.

Figure 122. Mound 83, Tomb 32 with capstones intact, and ring wall.

Figure 123. Mound 83, Tomb 44 with 3 jars.

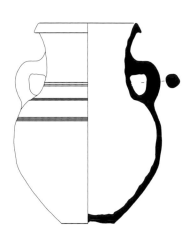

Figure 124. Type CQ Hard-fired ware jug from Mound 83-1985-86, Tomb 44.

Figure 125. Type 25 glass bottle from Mound 83-1985-86, Tomb 44.

Figure 126. Type 25 glass bottle from Mound 83-1985-86, Tomb 44.

Figure 127. Type 30 glass bottle from Mound 83-1985-86, Tomb 44.

Figure 129. Mound 83, Burial jar 2 in situ.

Figure 128. Mound 83, Tomb 52 after excavation. This tomb dates to the Dilmun period.

Figure 130. Type 15 glass bottle from Mound 83-1985-86, Jar 8.

Mound 84, 1985-86
Mustafa Ibrahim Salman

The excavation report from the excavation of this mound was lost in 2006, but the descriptions of the individual tombs were entered into a database in 2003. Only two tombs were found, one presumably dates to the Dilmun period and the other to the Tylos period. The Dilmun type tomb was surrounded by a low ring wall, and the walls of the Tylos period tomb were badly damaged. Neither tomb contained any finds.

Type	No	Trench	Built	Disturbed	Length	Width	Depth	Remarks
Tomb	1			Yes	220	53	7	
Tomb	2		On bedrock		221	78	81	Dilmun type.

Table 21. List of tombs (DS3 cemetery, Mound 84).

Figure 131. Mound 84 before excavation.

Figure 132. Mound 84 after excavation.

Figure 133. Section of Mound 84.

*Figure 134. Mound 8,
Tomb 1 with skeletal
remains.*

*Figure 135. Mound
84, Tomb 2, Dilmun
period tomb.*

Mound 88, 1985-86
Mustafa Ibrahim Salman

To the north of Mound 88 lay Mounds 73 and 74 at a distance of 9.5 m, to the south was Mound 91 at a distance of 11 m, and to the east was Mound 87 at a distance of 7 m. The area to the west was empty.

Mound 88 was round in shape and measured *c.* 11 m in diameter and had a height of 1.27 m above the surrounding terrain. The extension of the mound was, however, difficult to determine due to an uneven surface with depressions in the eastern half and gently sloping sides. The mound was covered with small stones.

The mound was excavated in four quadrants and no baulk was left between the excavation trenches.

Quadrant 1 was in the north-western section, Quadrant 2 in the south-west, Quadrant 3 in the south-east and Quadrant 4 in the north-east. The eastern part of the mound was the first to be excavated.

During the excavation, three tombs from the Tylos period were found. They were orientated north–south and were built on top of a Dilmun tomb in the centre of the mound. After the eastern part of the mound was excavated, the work continued in the western half to uncover the ring wall around the Dilmun grave. The Tylos tombs were also removed in order to clean the Dilmun tomb from above. The capstones of the Tylos tombs were robbed in antiquity. Below the mound was a layer of brown sand.

Type	No	Trench	Built	Disturbed	Length	Width	Depth	Remarks
Tomb	1		On bedrock	Yes	200	62		Dilmun type.
Tomb	2		Above bedrock	Yes	206	53	67	
Tomb	3		Above bedrock	Yes	204	51	63	
Tomb	4		Above bedrock	Yes	209	50	67	

Table 22. List of tombs (DS3 cemetery, Mound 88).

Type	No.	BNM No	Cat. no.	Material	Type	Number	Remark
Tomb	1	A14181		Pottery	Bead	3	
Tomb	2			Bronze	Spindle	1	
Tomb	2			Shell	N/A	1	
Tomb	3			Pottery	Bottle	1	
Tomb	3	A10566		Stone & glass	Bead	28	
Tomb	4	A4832	AP.23	Glazed pottery	Bowl	1	
Tomb	4			Ivory	Pin head	2	
Tomb	4	A4511	CL.9	Pottery	Bottle	1	

Table 23. List of finds (DS3 cemetery, Mound 88).

Figure 136. Cross section of Mound 88.

Figure 137. Mound 88 after excavation.

Figure 138. Mound 88, Tomb 1 dating to the Dilmun period.

Figure 139. Mound 88, Tomb 2 with skeletal remains.

Figure 140. Mound 88, Tomb 4 with skeletal remains.

Mound 135, 1985-86
Naseem Haider

The mound was situated within a residential complex. A road passed to the north of the mound. To the east, west and south there were houses at some distance.

The mound was badly damaged. It was oval in shape and orientated east–west. It measured c. 11 to 12 m across and had a height of 0.96 m above the surrounding terrain. The western half of the mound was higher than the eastern half and the surface of the mound was uneven. There were shallow pits in the top of the mound.

The slopes of the mound were gentle and almost flat to the southern side. Vehicles had severely damaged the slopes towards the east. The mound was covered with small stones.

The excavation of the mound was carried out in four quadrants and the mound was completely excavated. The filling of the mound consisted of brown sand and many small stones. Below the mound was a layer of brown pebbly sand, and in some places there were patches of grey soil. Sherds of glazed ware and grey ware were recovered from the mound fill in Quadrant 3, and four beads of semi-precious stones, two bronze finger rings, one bronze earring and a broken bronze bangle were recovered from the fill of Quadrant 1. A finger ring of green glass and some pieces of green glass bottles or jars were recovered from the fill of Quadrant 4. No finds from the tombs have been recorded.

During excavation, it was initially believed that eight tombs have been encountered but after removing the stones, it was found that the tombs numbered 3–7 were not tombs but remains of walls, probably from a house, and loose stones. Only three tombs were thus identified.[7]

Type	No	Trench	Built	Disturbed	Length	Width	Depth	Remarks
Tomb	1			Yes	205	62	36	
Tomb	2			Yes	121	52	31	
Tomb	8				142	51	27	

Table 24. List of tombs (DS3 cemetery, Mound 135).

[7] It is not clear from the evidence if the mound was a cemetery at all. The two sculls found in the mound fill are the only indications, but they could be from a disturbed tomb in the vicinity or a tomb pre-dating the walls. The walls look in fact more like the remains of a small house (see DS3 Mound 73 for a comparison). The finger ring made of green glass found in the mound fill of Quadrant 4 could indicate that the site is an Islamic settlement, since finger rings and bangles made of glass have not been noted in pre-Islamic contexts in Bahrain, but are common finds from Islamic sites.

Figure 141. Mound 135 before excavation.

Figure 142. First quadrant of Mound 135 excavated.

Figure 143. Mound 135 after excavation.

Figure 144. Mound 135, remains of walls in the centre of the mound.

Figure 145. Mound 135. Two sculls found in the mound fill near the centre of the mound.

Figure 146. Mound 135, Tombs 1 and 2 after excavation.

The Shakhoura Cemetery

Edited by Mustafa Ibrahim Salman

3

Mound 1, 1987
Abbas Ahmed

The mound measured 10 x 10 m and had a height of 0.9 m above the surroundings. It was round in shape, but was damaged on most sides. The mound was covered with small stones and soft sand.

For the excavation, the mound was divided into four quadrants, where Quadrant 1 was in the north-western section, Quadrant 2 in the south-west, Quadrant 3 in the south-east and Quadrant 4 in the north-east. No baulks were left between the trenches. The excavation began on the eastern part of the mound with Quadrants 3 and 4 and was completed before the western part was excavated.

Below the mound was bedrock and only one tomb was found. It was probably robbed in antiquity, since the capstones were missing and the grave lacked any finds. It was filled with sand and small stones, and was damaged in some parts.

Mound 1, 1987-88
Abbas Ahmed

This mound was located in the north-western area of Shakhoura in the centre of a group of unexcavated burial mounds. Two mounds lay 20 m away to the north-west and south-west respectively, and another mound lay 10 m away to the north.

Mound 1 measured 41 x 30 m and was rectangular. Bulldozers had damaged large parts of the mound in the northern and eastern parts, presumably to use the mound as fill at a nearby construction site. Consequently, some of the graves were exposed before the excavation began.

Quadrants measuring 5 x 5 m were laid out with 1 m-wide baulks in between. Excavation began with the highest parts of the mound and continued downwards. The mound fill consisted of small stones and soft sand and some pottery was found in the fill. Eleven tombs from the Tylos period were found at different levels in the mound.

Tomb 9 proved to be different from the standard Tylos tomb, since it had four rectangular pits of a depth of *c.* 15 cm in each corner of the floor of the tomb chamber. It was robbed from the north-west and south-west sides where parts of the walls were missing. It was filled with sand and contained one skeleton, a glazed pottery jar and one more vessel.

A statue of local stone was found in the fill in Square D5.

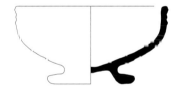

Figure 147. Type BA glazed pottery cup from Mound 1-1987-88, mound fill in Trench D4.

Type	No	Trench	Built	Disturbed	Length	Width	Depth	Remarks
Tomb	1		On bedrock	Yes	200	90	75	Empty.

Table 25. List of tomb (Shakhoura Cemetery, Mound 1-1987).

Mound 1, 1991-92
Abdul Kareem Jassem

Mound 1 was located in the south-western area of Shakhoura, and was surrounded by modern houses. The mound measured 29 m north–south and 23 m east–west and had an uneven surface with several pits. It was recently damaged in the northern and north-eastern parts.

The excavation was conducted in twenty squares measuring 5 x 5 m. There were 1 m-wide baulks left between the trenches. The excavation was continued until bedrock was reached and the baulks were removed at the end of the excavation. Tombs from the Dilmun period and the Tylos period were found and they varied in direction and size. Two ring walls were found in the south-eastern and north-western parts of the mound. In ring wall no. 1 (the south-eastern part of the mound), one tomb lay in the centre with a possible four tombs surrounding it. It is assumed that this central grave dated back to the Dilmun period, and in the Tylos period new tombs were placed in the periphery of the Bronze Age mound. Inside Ring wall no. 2 (the north-western part of the mound), three tombs were found. One tomb (no. 4) was of a different layout than the rest. It was orientated north–south and had two rooms to the east and west sides of the main chamber. This chamber was built of well-cut stone, which was held together by gypsum. As there was no capstone, the chamber was filled with sand and all that remained were a few human bones scattered around. Most of the graves were built on bedrock and had been robbed as the capstones and parts of the walls of the tombs were missing.

Type	No	Trench	Built	Disturbed	Length	Width	Depth	Remarks
Tomb	1	C5	On bedrock	Yes	196	70	100	Originally, three capstones but the one in the middle was robbed.
Tomb	2		On bedrock		234	67	96	
Tomb	3		On bedrock		214	70	90	
Tomb	4		On bedrock	Yes	205	67	96	Some capstones lost.
Tomb	5		On bedrock	Yes	210	73	95	
Tomb	6	B4	On bedrock	Yes	212	78	34	Some stones from the top of the wall lost and all capstones.
Tomb	7		On bedrock	Yes	208	59	63	
Tomb	8	E3	On bedrock		223	68	76	
Tomb	9	D3	On bedrock	Yes	200	68	97	
Tomb	10	E3	On bedrock	Yes	120	67	58	Some sections from the walls in the north lost.
Tomb	11	J2	On bedrock	Yes	212	66	37	Empty.

Table 26. List of tombs (Shakhoura Cemetery, Mound 1-1987-88).

Type	No.	BNM No.	Cat. no.	Material	Find type	Number	Remark
Tomb	2			Glazed pottery	Cup	1	Found outside tomb, upside down and with ash inside.
Tomb	4			Stone	Bead	1	
Tomb	5			Glazed pottery	Cup	1	Fragments, found outside tomb.
Tomb	7			Glazed pottery	Cup	1	Found outside tomb.
Tomb	8			Glazed pottery	Jar	1	
Tomb	8			Glazed pottery	Bowl	1	
Tomb	8			Stone	Bead	1	
Tomb	8	2235-2-90	BA.4	Glazed pottery	Cup	1	Fragments, found outside tomb.
Tomb	9	296	AE.4	Glazed pottery	Jar	1	
Tomb	9	4265-2-91-6	AP.11	Glazed pottery	Bowl	1	
Tomb	9			Glazed pottery	Cup	1	Found outside tomb, upside down and with ash inside.
Fill	0			Glazed pottery	Cup	1	Fragments, found outside tomb.
Fill	Tr. D4	2286-2-90	BA.9	Glazed pottery	Cup	1	Found outside tomb.
Fill	Tr. D5			Stone	Stele	1	

Table 27. List of finds (Shakhoura Cemetery, Mound 1-1987-88).

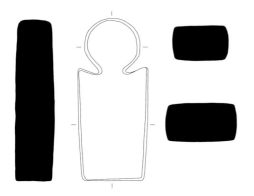 

25 cm

Figure 148. Anthropomorphic tombstone of the simple type found in the mound fill of Shakhoura, Mound 1-1991-92, Trench B6.

Figure 149. Anthropomorphic tombstone of the simple type found in the mound fill of Shakhoura, Mound 1-1991-92, Trench B6.

Type	No	Trench	Built	Disturbed	Length	Width	Depth	Remarks
Tomb	1		On bedrock	Yes	473	116	97	
Tomb	2	B1	On bedrock	Yes	206	77	40	
Tomb	3	B1	On bedrock		206	77	53	
Tomb	4	B2		Yes	741	205	66	
Tomb	5	B2	On bedrock	Yes	210	76	115	
Tomb	6	C1	On bedrock	Yes	140	49	46	
Tomb	7	C2	On bedrock	Yes	200	65	58	
Tomb	8	B2-B3	Into bedrock	Yes	175	90	95	
Tomb	9		On bedrock		198	56	58	
Tomb	10	B4	On bedrock	Yes	230	90	83	

Table 28. List of tombs (Shakhoura Cemetery, Mound 1-1991-92).

Type	No.	BNM No.	Cat. no.	Material	Find type	Number	Remark
Tomb	1			Pottery	Fragments		
Tomb	2			Pottery	Fragments		
Tomb	3			Pottery	Fragments		
Tomb	4			Pottery	Fragments		
Tomb	5			Pottery	Fragments		
Tomb	7			Glazed pottery	Bowl	1	
Tomb	8			Bronze	Fragments	1	
Tomb	8			Pottery	Bowl	1	Fragments.
Tomb	8			Pottery	Fragments		
Tomb	10	A9776		Stone	Bead	18	
Tomb	10			Alabaster	Bowl	1	
Tomb	10			N/A	Bowl	1	
Tomb	10			Alabaster	Bowl	1	Fragments.
Tomb	10			Seashell	N/A	1	
Tomb	10			Ivory	Pin head	4	
Tomb	10			Pottery	Figurine	1	Fragments.
Tomb	10			Glazed pottery	Bowl	1	Fragments.
Tomb	10			Seashell	Pin head	1	
Tomb	10			Bronze	Ring	1	
Fill		A11463		Stone	Statue	1	Trench B6

Table 29. List of finds (Shakhoura Cemetery, Mound 1-1991-92).

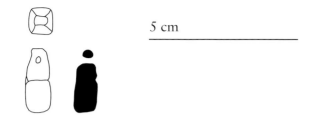

Figure 150. Rock crystal bead from Mound 1-1991-92, Tomb 10.

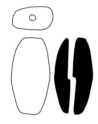

Figure 151. Bead made of mother-of-pearl from Mound 1-1991-92, Tomb 10.

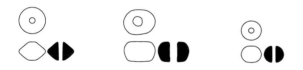

Figure 152. Glass beads from Mound 1-1991-92, Tomb 10.

Figure 153. Amethyst bead from Mound 1-1991-92, Tomb 10.

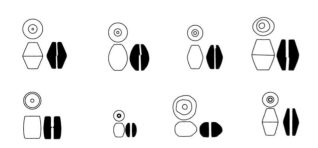

Figure 154. Carnelian beads from Mound 1-1991-92, Tomb 10.

Mound 1, 1992-93
Mustafa Ibrahim Salman

The mound was excavated to clear land for building private houses. To the west of the mound was the main road for Shakhoura village, to the north a mosque and to the east and south were private houses. The mound measured *c.* 65 x 47 m and had a maximum height of 2.79 m above the surroundings. The northern part of the mound was damaged, probably when the mosque was built or earlier.

The excavation started in October 1992 and was finished in March 1993. The excavation team consisted of about forty workers. The team was lead by Mustafa Ibrahim Salman, who was assisted by Abdul Kareem Jassim and Ali Juma. Qamees Ali executed the drawings and Saleh Ali took the photographs. The excavation started in the northern half of the mound where trenches, measuring 5 x 5 m and separated by 1 m-wide baulks, were laid out. After all the squares were excavated, the baulks were removed and the work continued in the southern part in a similar way. A 1 m-wide baulk was left in the centre of the mound during excavation to illustrate the section.

The excavation revealed seven burial jars and 187 tombs laid out in concentric circles around Tomb 69. One of the tombs (Tomb 62) dates to the Dilmun period. Eighty-six of the tombs showed signs of robbing in antiquity for both objects and building materials, twenty-six tombs had been robbed for objects, indicated by small openings in the structure, and stones (building material) were removed from twenty-nine tombs, without the grave goods having been disturbed. This leaves only forty-six tombs undisturbed.

In the south end of the mound a group of four anthropomorphic tombstones were found together in a niche in the ring wall. In front of the tombstones the foundation of a little structure was revealed, which measured *c.* 2 x 2 m and a few metres to the west traces of a fireplace were observed. A similar group of tombstones with a fireplace in front was found by Abdul Kareem and Abdul Hassan during excavations in the Al-Maqsha cemetery (unpublished).

Type	No	Trench	Built	Disturbed	Length	Width	Depth	Remarks
Tomb	1	A1	On bedrock	Yes	195	48	56	4 pits in each corner of the floor.
Tomb	2		On bedrock	Yes	208	64	80	
Tomb	3		On bedrock	Yes	212	68	100	
Tomb	4	A2	Above bedrock		97	46	53	
Tomb	5	A2	Above bedrock		76	33	35	Not plastered inside. Two courses of unworked stones.
Tomb	6	A2	Above bedrock	Yes	204	46	56	
Tomb	7	B3	On bedrock	Yes	182	66	107	
Tomb	8		On bedrock	Yes	219	32	86	
Tomb	9		On bedrock	Yes	207	38	83	
Tomb	10		On bedrock	Yes	187	56	100	
Tomb	11		On bedrock	Yes	175	55	65	
Tomb	12		On bedrock	Yes	201	63	97	
Tomb	13		On bedrock	Yes	214	72	97	
Tomb	14		On bedrock		208	59	112	
Tomb	15	C3	On bedrock		216	61	79	
Tomb	16	D3	Above bedrock	Yes	206	70	105	
Tomb	17		Above bedrock	Yes	100	40	62	Empty.
Tomb	18		Above bedrock	Yes	170	43	13	Empty.
Tomb	19		On bedrock	Yes	200	69	103	
Tomb	20		On bedrock	Yes	203	73	17	
Tomb	21		On bedrock	Yes	192	51	57	
Tomb	22		Above bedrock	Yes	203	58	99	
Tomb	23		On bedrock	Yes	104	59	38	
Tomb	24		Above bedrock	Yes	109	60	71	Empty.
Tomb	25		On bedrock	Yes	183	44	59	
Tomb	26	AA2	On bedrock	Yes	189	53	49	Empty?
Tomb	27		On bedrock	Yes	140	60	51	
Tomb	28		On bedrock		210	70	127	Findings reconstructed from find database and map.
Tomb	29		On bedrock	Yes	206	58	100	
Tomb	30		On bedrock		195	61	75	Empty
Tomb	31		On bedrock		200	69	113	
Tomb	32		On bedrock	Yes	196	63	22	
Tomb	33		On bedrock	Yes	213	69	118	
Tomb	34	C4	Above bedrock		217	65	115	Footprint in the mortar of the frame.
Tomb	35	B4	On bedrock	Yes	214	65	115	
Tomb	36							No information.
Tomb	37		On bedrock	Yes	205	65	115	
Tomb	38		On bedrock		217	62	115	
Tomb	39		On bedrock		205	64	121	
Tomb	40		Above bedrock		208	61	79	
Tomb	41		On bedrock	Yes	208	64	114	
Tomb	42		Above bedrock	Yes	225	67	113	
Tomb	43	A5	On bedrock	Yes	203	53	60	
Tomb	44	AA5	Above bedrock		180	46	47	
Tomb	45		Above bedrock	Yes	218	66	112	
Tomb	46		Above bedrock	Yes	226	73	120	Empty.
Tomb	47		On bedrock	Yes	204	69	98	
Tomb	48	C5	Above bedrock	Yes	202	41	54	
Tomb	49		On bedrock	Yes	190	46	46	
Tomb	50		Above bedrock	Yes	202	46	43	Empty.
Tomb	51	B7	Above bedrock	Yes	65	35	25	
Tomb	52		On bedrock	Yes	60	30	30	Empty.

Type	No	Trench	Built	Disturbed	Length	Width	Depth	Remarks
Tomb	102		Above bedrock	Yes	88	40	64	
Tomb	103			Yes	190	45	36	Empty, and only floor and max. 36 cm of wall preserved.
Tomb	104		Above bedrock	Yes	115	63	100	
Tomb	105		Above bedrock	Yes	200	45	91	
Tomb	106		Above bedrock	Yes	204	57	100	
Tomb	107		Above bedrock	Yes	65	34	33	Empty.
Tomb	108		Above bedrock		68	30	38	
Tomb	109		Above bedrock	Yes	224	69	110	Empty.
Tomb	110		Above bedrock	Yes	205	53	89	
Tomb	111		Above bedrock	Yes	216	66	39	
Tomb	112		Above bedrock	Yes	237	67	71	Empty.
Tomb	113		On bedrock		206	60	92	
Tomb	114		Above bedrock	Yes	213	58	99	Empty.
Tomb	115		Above bedrock	Yes	171	62	77	Empty.
Tomb	116		Above bedrock	Yes	216	61	99	
Tomb	117		Above bedrock	Yes	191	52	61	Empty.
Tomb	118		Above bedrock	Yes	203	61	96	
Tomb	119		Above bedrock		194	61	52	Empty.
Tomb	120	F2	Above bedrock	Yes	208	66	107	
Tomb	121	F2	Above bedrock		208	61	97	
Tomb	122	F1	Above bedrock		110	60	50	
Tomb	123	F1	On bedrock	Yes	184	52	52	
Tomb	124	F1	Above bedrock	Yes	190	46	55	
Tomb	125		Above bedrock	Yes	211	40	44	
Tomb	126		Above bedrock	Yes	163	57	85	Empty.
Tomb	127		Above bedrock	Yes	200	40	60	Empty.
Tomb	128		Above bedrock	Yes	207	51	57	Empty.
Tomb	129		Above bedrock	Yes	185	61		Only floor.
Tomb	130		Above bedrock	Yes	210	70	80	Empty.
Tomb	131		Above bedrock	Yes	235	62	117	Empty.
Tomb	132		Above bedrock		203	44	49	Half of Dilmun jar found upside down outside grave.
Tomb	134		Above bedrock	Yes	200	58	56	
Tomb	135		Above bedrock	Yes	230	68	120	
Tomb	136		Above bedrock		227	65	117	
Tomb	137		Above bedrock	Yes	229	74	124	Empty.
Tomb	138		Above bedrock		211	60	87	
Tomb	139		Above bedrock	Yes	211	66	116	
Tomb	140	G2	Above bedrock	Yes	226	70	125	Empty?
Tomb	141		On bedrock	Yes	202	75	85	Empty.
Tomb	142			Yes	213	50	54	Empty.
Tomb	143		Above bedrock	Yes	200	49	30	Empty.
Tomb	144		Above bedrock		189	52	53	1 pit across in the south end.
Tomb	145		On bedrock	Yes	216	62	93	
Tomb	146	G6	Above bedrock	Yes	205	50	51	
Tomb	147		On bedrock	Yes	191	48	42	
Tomb	148		On bedrock	Yes	210	77	53	Empty.
Tomb	149		Above bedrock	Yes	103	45	51	Empty.
Tomb	150		Above bedrock	Yes	71	37	40	Empty. Stone slabs uncut.
Tomb	151		Above bedrock	Yes	212	44	53	Empty.
Tomb	152		Above bedrock		93	34	56	
Tomb	153		Above bedrock	Yes	216	64	89	Empty.

Type	No	Trench	Built	Disturbed	Length	Width	Depth	Remarks
Tomb	154		Above bedrock	Yes	225	69	113	Empty.
Tomb	155		Above bedrock	Yes	221	66	87	Empty.
Tomb	156		Above bedrock		209	63	108	
Tomb	157		Above bedrock	Yes	221	62	91	Empty. 1 pit across in west end.
Tomb	158		Above bedrock	Yes	200	48	55	Empty.
Tomb	159		Above bedrock		183	47	49	1 pit across in west end.
Tomb	160		On bedrock	Yes	195	46	51	Empty.
Tomb	161		Above bedrock	Yes	91	46	48	Empty.
Tomb	162		Above bedrock	Yes	189	47	51	Empty.
Tomb	163		Above bedrock	Yes	193	50	51	Empty. 1 pit across in south end.
Tomb	164		Above bedrock	Yes	0			Empty. 1 pit across in west end.
Tomb	165		Above bedrock	Yes	197	57		
Tomb	166		Above bedrock		210	43	45	Tomb contained material, but some information lost. (Restored)
Tomb	167		Above bedrock	Yes	208	43	60	Empty. 1 trench across in west end.
Tomb	168		Above bedrock	Yes	78	65	16	Empty.
Tomb	169	H4			0			Information lost.
Tomb	170				0			All information lost. Finds reconstructed from find database and photos.
Tomb	171		Above bedrock	Yes	186	47	46	Empty.
Tomb	172			Yes	71	36	40	Empty.
Tomb	173		Above bedrock	Yes	172	49	47	Empty.
Tomb	174	I3	Above bedrock	Yes	190	48	47	
Tomb	175	I3	On bedrock	Yes	113	47	57	The find information is probably mixed with tomb 174, however, Figure 220 and the find registration indicate that the information belongs to this grave. A wall was built across the tomb in order to facilitate a child burial.
Tomb	176	G5	Above bedrock	Yes	200	47	53	1 pit across in the south end.
Tomb	177		Above bedrock	Yes	202	50	58	1 pit across in the west end. Empty.
Tomb	178		On bedrock	Yes	102	47	39	Empty.
Tomb	179		Above bedrock	Yes	198	44	49	
Tomb	180		Above bedrock	Yes	194	50	116	Empty.
Tomb	181	I3	Above bedrock		211	46	46	1 pit across in west end.
Tomb	182		Above bedrock	Yes	200	62	95	
Tomb	183		Above bedrock	Yes	189	51	51	Empty.
Tomb	184			Yes	192	53	13	Empty.
Tomb	185	H6	On bedrock		108	46	58	Bones from first burial pushed aside to facilitate second burial.
Tomb	186		Above bedrock	Yes	193	47	45	
Tomb	187			Yes	180	49	43	Empty.
Tomb	188		Above bedrock		171	53	71	

Table 30. List of tombs (Shakhoura Cemetery, Mound 1-1992-93).

Type	No	Trench	Length	Max. Ø	Rim Ø	Remarks
Jar	1	A3	60	38	29	
Jar	2	C5	56	45	27	
Jar	3	D8	63	37	23	
Jar	4	I3	43	34	11	Empty.
Jar	5	G3	47	38	17	
Jar	6	G2				
Jar	7	F5	52	39	22	

Table 31. List of burials jars (Shakhoura Cemetery, Mound 1-1992-93).

Type	No.	BNM No.	Cat. no.	Material	Find type	Number	Remark
Tomb	1	A13231		Bronze	Spatula	2	
Tomb	1	43	AQ.34	Glazed pottery	Bowl	1	
Tomb	1	A9892		Iron	Dagger	1	
Tomb	3	A12964		Bronze	N/A	1	
Tomb	3	A12964		Bronze	Coin	1	
Tomb	4	A13027		Stone	Bead	5	
Tomb	4			Glass	Bottle	1	
Tomb	4	A11554		Seashell	Bottom	1	
Tomb	5	A11096		Seashell	N/A	6	
Tomb	5	A13327		Bronze	Bangle	1	
Tomb	5	12	BO.19	Glazed pottery	Little pot	1	
Tomb	5	A11551		Ivory	Pin	1	
Tomb	5	A13132		Stone	Bead		Many.
Tomb	5	A16087		Bronze	N/A	1	
Tomb	6	A12977		Bronze	Coin	1	
Tomb	7	A12516		Ivory	Pin		
Tomb	7			Pottery	Bowl	1	Found outside tomb.
Tomb	9			Pottery	Incense burner	1	Found outside tomb.
Tomb	13			Pottery	Fragments		
Tomb	13	47	AQ.24	Glazed pottery	Bowl	1	
Tomb	13	A227	BL.31	Glazed pottery	Jar	1	
Tomb	13			Bronze	Ladle	1	
Tomb	13			Bronze	N/A		
Tomb	13	3924-2-91-6-1640-377	BF.29	Glazed pottery	Cup	1	
Tomb	14	48	AQ.114	Glazed pottery	Bowl	1	
Tomb	14	A1058		Bronze	Ladle	1	
Tomb	15	97	BN.4	Glazed pottery	Bottle	1	
Tomb	15	A11553		Ivory	Pin head	6	
Tomb	15	A11555		Ivory	Pin		Fragments.
Tomb	15	A12965		Bronze	Coin	1	
Tomb	16	121	BF.52	Glazed pottery	Cup	1	Found outside tomb.
Tomb	19			Pottery	N/A		
Tomb	19	A10518		Glass	Bead	1	
Tomb	21			Pottery	Bowl	1	
Tomb	25			Ivory	Pin head	2	
Tomb	25			Bitumen	Basket	1	Fragments.
Tomb	25			Bone	N/A		
Tomb	25			Bronze	Pin head	1	
Tomb	26	10	AQ.102	Glazed pottery	Bowl	1	
Tomb	26	A9535	19.1	Glass	Bottle	1	
Tomb	26	A12652		Stone & glass	Bead	30	
Tomb	26	A13283		Bronze	Pin	1	
Tomb	26			Glass	Bottle	1	
Tomb	26	A12538		Stone	Pin head	2	One with remnants of an iron pin.
Tomb	26	A13227		Bronze	Spatula	1	
Tomb	26	A12652		Glass	Bead		Many.
Tomb	27			Bronze	N/A		
Tomb	28	126	BM.8	Glazed pottery	Jug	1	

Type	No.	BNM No.	Cat. no.	Material	Find type	Number	Remark
Tomb	28	127-1768	AQ.91	Glazed pottery	Bowl	1	
Tomb	29	91-1-38	BA.14	Glazed pottery	Cup	1	
Tomb	29	115	BL.2	Glazed pottery	Jar	1	
Tomb	29			Iron	Dagger	1	
Tomb	29			Bronze	Ring	1	
Tomb	29	116	AQ.19	Glazed pottery	Bowl	1	
Tomb	31			Glass	Bowl	1	
Tomb	31	A11559		Ivory	Pin head	1	
Tomb	33			Pottery	N/A		
Tomb	34			Wood	Coffin	1	
Tomb	35	A195	NON.52	Pottery	Incense burner	1	
Tomb	36	A9894		Iron	Tool	1	
Tomb	37			Glazed pottery	Bowl	1	Fragments.
Tomb	37			Pottery	Bowl	1	Fragments.
Tomb	40	5	X.3	Pottery	Bowl	1	Found outside tomb.
Tomb	41			Pottery	Bowl	1	
Tomb	42	120	BF.43	Glazed pottery	Cup	1	Found outside tomb.
Tomb	42	A10222		Ivory	Cosmetic container	1	
Tomb	42			Seashell	N/A	1	
Tomb	43	A13240		Bronze	Pin		Fragments.
Tomb	43			Pottery	Bottle	1	
Tomb	43			Pottery	Bowl	1	Fragments.
Tomb	44	A13781		Bronze	Spatula	1	
Tomb	44			Pottery	N/A		
Tomb	47			Pottery	N/A		
Tomb	48			Pottery	Bowl	1	Fragments.
Tomb	49	A12951		Stone	Bead	2	
Tomb	51	A9059	7.1	Glass	Bottle	1	Fragments.
Tomb	51			Seashell	N/A	1	
Tomb	51			Bronze	Bracelet	1	
Tomb	51	A10519		Stone	Bead	5	
Tomb	53	A16050		Bronze	Bead	1	
Tomb	55			Pottery	Bowl	1	
Tomb	56			Pottery	Bottle	1	Fragments.
Tomb	56	A12992		Stone & bronze	Bead	3	
Tomb	57	2	AQ.50	Pottery	Bowl	1	
Tomb	58			Bronze	N/A		
Tomb	58	A12975		Stone	Bead	3	
Tomb	62			Pottery	Jar	2	
Tomb	62			Seashell	N/A	3	
Tomb	62			Bronze	N/A		
Tomb	62			Stone	Dilmun seal	1	
Tomb	67			Glazed pottery	Cup	1	Found outside tomb.
Tomb	72			Ivory	Pin head	1	
Tomb	72			Bronze	Pin	1	
Tomb	72			Stone	Bead	N/A	
Tomb	72	84	AT.2	Glazed pottery	Bowl	1	
Tomb	72			Seashell	N/A	1	

Type	No.	BNM No.	Cat. no.	Material	Find type	Number	Remark
Tomb	72			Bronze	N/A	0	
Tomb	75	A11038	15.2	Glass	Bottle	1	
Tomb	75	A12969		Bronze	Bangle	1	
Tomb	75	A12968		Bronze	Spatula	1	
Tomb	75	A13128		Stone	Bead	27	
Tomb	75			Bronze	N/A	1	
Tomb	75			Seashell	N/A	1	
Tomb	77			Ivory	Pin head	1	
Tomb	80	A12474		Ivory	Pin		Fragments.
Tomb	81	A13180		Glass	Bead	3	
Tomb	81	A12472		Stone	N/A	3	Yellow stone.
Tomb	82			Pottery	Bowl		Fragments.
Tomb	84	191	AT.5	Glazed pottery	Bowl	1	
Tomb	84			Bronze	Bangle	2	
Tomb	84			Seashell	N/A	2	
Tomb	84	A13377		Bronze	Spatula	1	Fragments.
Tomb	84			Bronze	Ring	1	
Tomb	84			Stone	Bead	N/A	
Tomb	88			Bronze	Fragments		
Tomb	88	A12491		Ivory	Pin head	14	
Tomb	88	A12970		Silver	Finger ring	2	
Tomb	88	A13238		Bronze	Spatula	2	
Tomb	88			Stone	N/A	1	
Tomb	88			Seashell	N/A	1	
Tomb	88	A12446		Glass	Bead	10	
Tomb	91	113	AF.25	Glazed pottery	Cup	1	Fragments.
Tomb	94			Glazed pottery	Jar	1	
Tomb	94	141	AQ.89	Glazed pottery	Bowl	1	Fragments.
Tomb	94			Iron	Dagger	1	Fragments.
Tomb	99	N/A		Iron	Fragments	N/A	Found outside tomb.
Tomb	101			Seashell	N/A	2	
Tomb	101			Stone	N/A	1	
Tomb	102	A9773		Stone	Bead	403	
Tomb	102	A13334		Bronze	Earring	2	
Tomb	102	A13237		Bronze	Coin	1	
Tomb	102	A13153		Ivory	Pin head	4	
Tomb	102	53	BE.21	Glazed pottery	Cup	1	Found outside tomb.
Tomb	102	A13236		Bronze	Spatula		Fragments.
Tomb	104	A13178		Pottery	Seal impression	1	
Tomb	105	130	BE.33	Glazed pottery	Cup	1	Found outside tomb, fragments.
Tomb	108	139	AY.3	Glazed pottery	Small bowl	1	
Tomb	108	136	AQ.18	Glazed pottery	Bowl	1	
Tomb	108	A336	13.13	Glass	Bottle	1	
Tomb	108			Glass	Bottle	1	
Tomb	111	152	BY.1	Glazed pottery	Bottle	1	
Tomb	111	151	AO.7	Glazed pottery	Bowl	1	Fragments.
Tomb	120	160	BE.70	Glazed pottery	Cup	1	
Tomb	121	A13973		Stone	Bead	40	29 in store.
Tomb	121	A12494		Ivory & stone	Pin head	8	

Type	No.	BNM No.	Cat. no.	Material	Find type	Number	Remark
Tomb	121	A13228		Iron	Dagger	1	
Tomb	121	174	BL.6	Glazed pottery	Jar	1	
Tomb	121	A13229		Bronze	Spatula	1	
Tomb	121			Bone	N/A	31	
Tomb	121			Bronze	Ring	1	
Tomb	121	173	BQ.3	Glazed pottery	Bottle	1	
Tomb	122			Glass	Bottle	1	
Tomb	122	A12967		Bronze	Spatula	1	
Tomb	123	A8928	13.1	Glass	Bottle	1	
Tomb	123	133	AQ.60	Glazed pottery	Bowl	1	Fragments.
Tomb	123	A13230		Bronze	Spatula	1	
Tomb	123	134	BE.53	Glazed pottery	Cup	1	Fragments.
Tomb	124	155	AQ.20	Glazed pottery	Bowl	1	
Tomb	124	A12972		Bronze	Bead	3	
Tomb	132			Pottery	Dilmun	1	Found outside tomb, fragments.
Tomb	134	A13224		Bronze	Pin	1	
Tomb	134	A12351		Ivory	Pin head	1	
Tomb	134	134	AH.42	Glazed pottery	Bowl	1	Fragments.
Tomb	135	164	AH.4	Glazed pottery	Bowl	1	Found outside tomb, fragments.
Tomb	136	172	AQ.54	Glazed pottery	Bowl	1	Fragments.
Tomb	136	170	AQ.16	Glazed pottery	Bowl	1	
Tomb	136		BF.5	Glazed pottery	Cup	1	
Tomb	138		BM.10	Glazed pottery	Jug	1	Fragments.
Tomb	138		DH.2	Pottery	Basket	1	Fragments.
Tomb	140	A12973		Bronze	Coin	1	
Tomb	144			Bronze	Fragments	1	
Tomb	145			Iron	Dagger	1	Fragments.
Tomb	146	149	CV.3	Glazed pottery	Small bowl	1	
Tomb	146			Iron	Nails	N/A	
Tomb	147	145	AQ.111	Glazed pottery	Bowl	1	Fragments.
Tomb	152	205	BZ.5	Glazed pottery	Bottle	1	Fragments.
Tomb	152			Seashell	Bead	6	
Tomb	152	A14075		Stone	Signet	1	
Tomb	156	238	AQ.98	Glazed pottery	Bowl	1	
Tomb	156			Bronze	Pin	1	
Tomb	165			Glazed pottery	Bowl	1	
Tomb	165			Glass	Bottle	N/A	Fragments.
Tomb	166	A13234		Bronze	Pin	1	
Tomb	166	161	BC.8	Glazed pottery	Cup	1	Found outside tomb, with ash inside.
Tomb	166	218	AQ.110	Glazed pottery	Bowl	1	
Tomb	166	A9536	15.7	Glass	Bottle	1	
Tomb	166			Glazed pottery	Bottle	1	
Tomb	166			Stone	Bead	77	
Tomb	169	216	BF.12	Glazed pottery	Cup	1	
Tomb	169	215	AQ.52	Glazed pottery	Bowl	1	
Tomb	169	211	BR.4	Glazed pottery	Bottle	1	
Tomb	170	163	BE.11	Glazed pottery	Cup	1	
Tomb	170	166	AQ.81	Glazed pottery	Bowl	1	
Tomb	170	A9529	15.8	Glass	Bottle	1	

Type	No.	BNM No.	Cat. no.	Material	Find type	Number	Remark
Tomb	170	A11260	18.6	Glass	Bottle	1	
Tomb	170	A11184		Stone	Pin head	1	
Tomb	175	217	AQ.85	Glazed pottery	Bowl	1	
Tomb	175	A9514	11.2	Glass	Bottle	1	
Tomb	175	A12653		Stone	Bead	61	
Tomb	175	A13235		Bronze	Spatula	1	
Tomb	175	153	BC.4	Glazed pottery	Cup	1	Found outside tomb, fragments.
Tomb	175	A9515	11.1	Glass	Bottle	1	
Tomb	175	A11037	6.2	Glass	Bottle	1	
Tomb	175	A8932	15.1	Glass	Bottle	1	
Tomb	176	157	BC.7	Glazed pottery	Cup	1	Found outside tomb, fragments.
Tomb	176	A12971		Bronze	Coin	1	
Tomb	179	A15874		Iron	Dagger	1	Fragments.
Tomb	181	203	AQ.93	Glazed pottery	Bowl	1	
Tomb	181	A13847		Bronze	Fragments	N/A	
Tomb	185	239	AQ.55	Glazed pottery	Bowl	1	Fragments.
Jar	1			Stone	Bead	N/A	
Jar	1			Bone	Infant	1	Fragments.
Jar	2			Bone	Infant	1	Fragments.
Jar	2			Stone	Bead	N/A	
Jar	2			Seashell	N/A	3	
Jar	3			Seashell	N/A	2	
Jar	5	229	BO.15	Glazed pottery	Cosmetic pot	1	
Jar	5			Bone	Infant	1	Fragments.
Jar	5	A13145		Glass	Bead	1	
Jar	5	A13145		Bronze	Bead	1	
Jar	5	A13145		Stone	Bead	1	
Jar	7	A13133		Stone	Bead		Many.
Jar	7	A13133		Bronze & stone	Bead	29	
Fill				Pottery	Cup	1	
Fill				Stone	Mortar and grinder	2	
Fill				Glazed pottery	Cup	1	Fragments, with ash inside.
Fill				Stone	Grinder	1	
Fill		A11465 A11450		Stone	Stele	4	Trench J3
Fill		4	BF.66	Glazed pottery	Cup	1	Fragments.
Jar	6	A11656		Stone	Bead		Many.
Jar	6	A11656		Glass & stone	Bead	28	

Table 32. List of finds (Shakhoura Cemetery, Mound 1-1992-93).

Figure 155. Mound 1-1992-93 before excavation.

Figure 156. Mound 1-1992-93 during excavation.

Figure 157. Mound 1-1992-93 after excavation.

Figure 159. Four tombstones together with one roughly shaped stone were found together in a niche in the retaining wall which can be seen in the centre of the photo (Mound 1-1992-93, Trench J3).

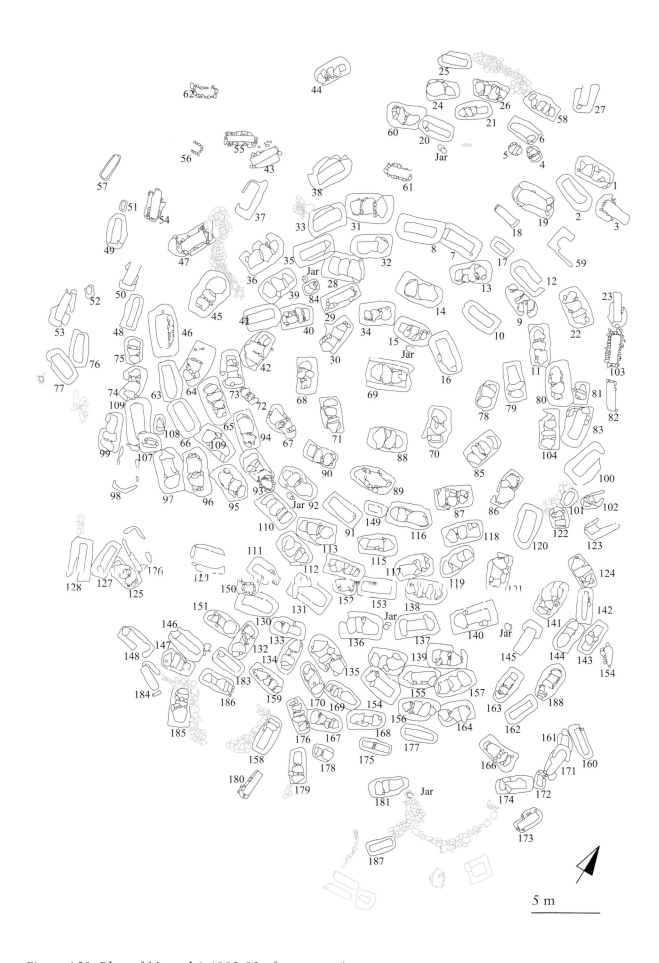

Figure 158. Plan of Mound 1-1992-93 after excavation.

Figure 160. Four tombstones found in the edge of Mound 1-1992-93.

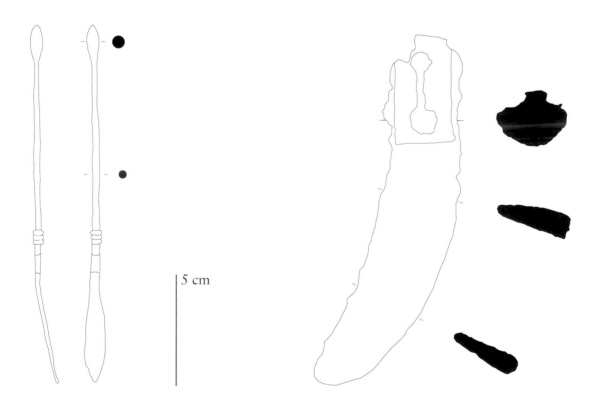

5 cm

Figure 165. Spatula made of bronze from Mound 1-1992-93, Tomb 1.

Figure 166. Iron tool with remnants of a wooden handle from Mound 1-1992-93, Tomb 1.

Figure 161. Three of the anthropomorphic tombstones found in Mound 1-1992-93, Trench J3.

Figure 162. Tombstone found in the edge of Mound 1-1992-93.

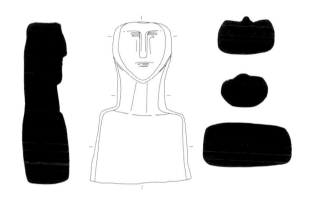

Figure 163. Tombstone found in the edge of Mound 1-1992-93.

25 cm

Figure 164. Tombstone found in the edge of Mound 1-1992-93.

Figure 167. Type AQ glazed ware bowl from Mound 1-1992-93, Tomb 1.

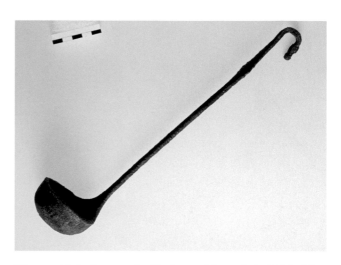

Figure 170. Bronze ladle from Mound 1-1992-93, Tomb 14.

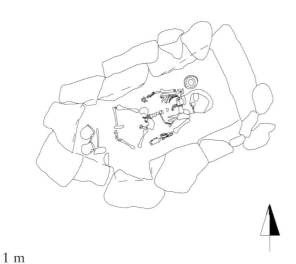

1 m

Figure 168. Plan of Mound 1-1992-93, Tomb 5 after excavation.

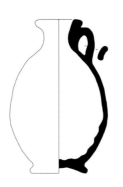

Figure 171. Type BN glazed ware jug from Mound 1-1992-93, Tomb 15.

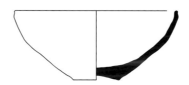

Figure 172. Type AQ glazed ware bowl from Mound 1-1992-93, Tomb 26.

Figure 169. Type AQ glazed ware bowl from Mound 1-1992-93, Tomb 14.

Figure 173. Type 19 glass bottle from Mound 1-1992-93, Tomb 26.

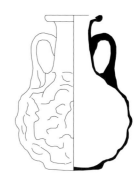

Figure 174. Type 19 glass bottle from Mound 1-1992-93, Tomb 26.

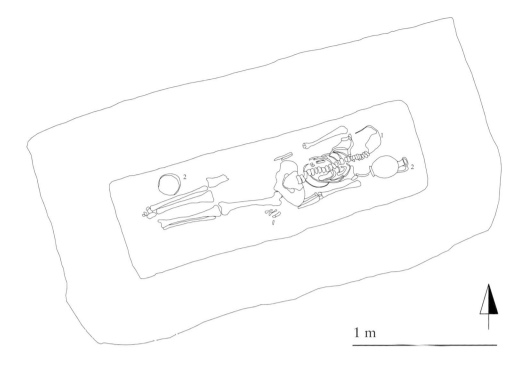

Figure 175. Plan of Mound 1-1992-93, Tomb 28 after excavation.

Figure 176. Type AQ glazed ware bowl from Mound 1-1992-93, Tomb 29.

Figure 177. "Pin head" made of ivory from Mound 1-1992-93, Tomb 31.

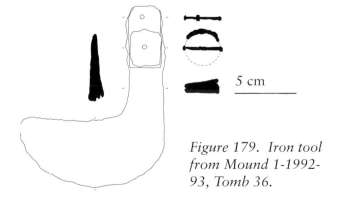

Figure 179. Iron tool from Mound 1-1992-93, Tomb 36.

Figure 178. Mound 1-1992-93, Tomb 34 with remains of a wooden coffin and footprint in the mortar of the frame.

Figure 180. Mound 1-1992-93, Tomb 51.

Figure 181. Type
7 glass bottle from
Mound 1-1992-93,
Tomb 51.

Figure 183. Mound 1-1992-93, Tomb 71.

Figure 182. Type AQ glazed ware bowl
from Mound 1-1992-93, Tomb 57.

Figure 184. Type AT glazed ware bowl
from Mound 1-1992-93, Tomb 72.

Figure 185. Type
15 glass bottle from
Mound 1-1992-93,
Tomb 75.

Figure 186. Type 15
glass bottle from Mound
1-1992-93, Tomb 75.

Figure 187. Mound 1-1992-93, Tomb 84.

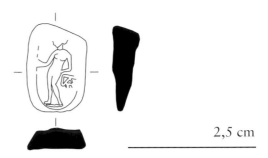

2,5 cm

Figure 190. Seal impression in clay from Mound 1-1992-93, Tomb 104.

Figure 188. Type AT glazed ware bowl from Mound 1-1992-93, Tomb 84.

Figure 191. Photo of seal impression in clay from Mound 1-1992-93, Tomb 104.

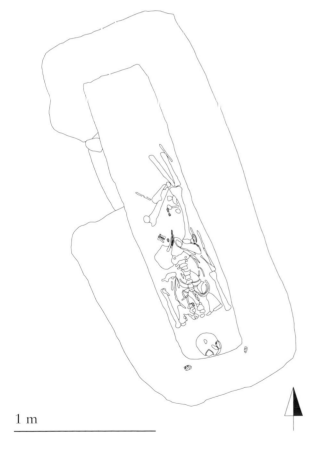

Figure 192. Mound 1-1992-93, Tomb 108 with grave goods.

Figure 193. Type AY glazed ware bowl from Mound 1-1992-93, Tomb 108.

1 m

Figure 189. Plan of Mound 1-1992-93, Tomb 99 after excavation. In the southern part of the plaster surrounding the chamber two iron nails can be observed.

Figure 213. Type AQ glazed ware bowl from Mound 1-1992-93, Tomb 169.

Figure 211. Type
15 glass bot-
tle from Mound
1-1992-93, Tomb
166.

Figure 212. Type
15 glass bottle from
Mound 1-1992-93,
Tomb 166.

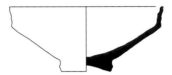

Figure 214. Type BF glazed ware cup from
Mound 1-1992-93, Tomb 169.

Figure 215. Glazed ware cup placed upside down
on the top of the capstones of Mound 1-1992-93,
Tomb 170.

Figure 216. Mound 1-1992-93, Tomb 170 with
grave goods.

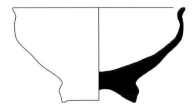

Figure 217. Type BE glazed ware bowl from Mound 1-1992-93, Tomb 170.

Figure 218. Type 18 glass bottle from Mound 1-1992-93, Tomb 170.

Figure 219. Type 18 glass bottle from Mound 1-1992-93, Tomb 170.

Figure 220. Mound 1-1992-93, Tomb 175 modified with a drystone wall to accommodate the burial of a child.

Figure 221. Type 11 glass bottle from Mound 1-1992-93, Tomb 175.

Figure 222. Type 11 glass bottle from Mound 1-1992-93, Tomb 175.

Figure 223. Type 11 glass bottle from Mound 1-1992-93, Tomb 175.

Figure 224. Type
6 glass bottle from
Mound 1-1992-93,
Tomb 175.

Figure 225. Type
6 glass bottle from
Mound 1-1992-93,
Tomb 175.

Figure 226. Type
15 glass bottle from
Mound 1-1992-93,
Tomb 175.

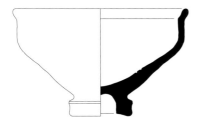

Figure 227. Type BC glazed ware
cup from Mound 1-1992-93,
Tomb 175.

Figure 228. Mound 1-1992-93, Tomb 185.
The bones from first burial were pushed aside
to facilitate a second burial.

Mound 1, 1994-95
Mustafa Ibrahim Salman

Mound 1 was located in the western part of the Shakhoura cemetery. There were burial mounds lying to the north and west, and modern houses to the south and east of the mound.

The mound measured 25 m north–south and 13 m east–west. It had a height of 2.2 m above the surroundings. The surface was uneven and the mound had a very steep slope to the south-west. There were also pits in different parts of the mound.

The mound was divided into trenches measuring 12 x 5 m. Baulks 1 m wide were initially left between the trenches, but removed at the end of the excavation. Nine tombs and one burial jar were found, and one pottery vessel and one tombstone were recovered in the mound fill. The tombs appear to have been built on two levels, which may have a chronological significance. On the lower level the tombs were built on the bedrock, whereas on the upper level, the tombs were built on the ancient surface or in the mound fill. Tombs 2, 3 and 9 were on the lower level and Tombs 1, 4, 5, 6, 7 and 8 were on the upper level.

All graves belonged to the Tylos period and had their walls plastered, which was normal for the Tylos period tombs. Tombs 2, 5 and 9 were orientated east–west and Tombs 3, 6, 7 and 8 were orientated north–south. Tomb 4 was orientated in a north-west–south-east direction. Most of the tombs did not have capstones, were empty, and therefore presumably robbed in antiquity. Tomb 1 was destroyed and could not even be measured.

Tombs 3 and 8 contained a few bones. Tomb 2 contained two well-preserved moulded plaster figurines and the remains of a third plaster figurine, and the skeleton of an adult.

Type	No	Trench	Built	Disturbed	Length	Width	Depth	Remarks
Tomb	1	C1		Yes				Grave destroyed.
Tomb	2	C2	On bedrock	Yes	220	56	69	
Tomb	3	D2	Above bedrock	Yes	204	57	94	
Tomb	4	D1	Above bedrock	Yes	220	70	85	Empty.
Tomb	5	D1	Above bedrock	Yes	220	72	70	Empty.
Tomb	6	E1	Above bedrock	Yes	216	67	97	Empty.
Tomb	7	B1	Above bedrock	Yes	212	69	110	Empty.
Tomb	8	B1	Above bedrock	Yes	210	68	83	
Tomb	9	A2	On bedrock	Yes	208	61	53	Empty.

Table 33. List of tombs (Shakhoura Cemetery, Mound 1-1994-95).

Type	No	Trench	Length	Max. Ø	Rim Ø	Remarks
Jar	1	D2	77	42	16	

Table 34. List of burial jars (Shakhoura Cemetery, Mound 1-1994-95).

Type	No.	BNM No.	Cat. no.	Material	Find type	Number	Remark
Tomb	2			Plaster	Figurine	3	
Fill		A9820		Stone	Statue	1	

Table 35. List of finds (Shakhoura Cemetery, Mound 1-1994-95).

25 cm

Figure 229. Anthropomorphic tombstone of the simple type found in the mound fill of Mound 1-1994-95.

Figure 230. Anthropomorphic tombstone of the simple type found in the mound fill of Mound 1-1994-95.

Figure 231. Moulded plaster figurines, Mound 1-1994-95, Tomb 2.

Mound A1, 1996-97

Mustafa Ibrahim Salman

The development of Shakhoura village required the removal of the mound to clear land to build private houses. The mound was situated between the road from Shakhoura to the Budaiya road, a garden, the Shakhoura Centre and private houses. It measured *c*. 80 x 50 m and had a maximum height of *c*. 4 m above the surrounding terrain and 12.7 m above sea level. A cut in the eastern part of the mound suggests that the mound was bigger in antiquity, but it is still one of the largest mounds that has ever been excavated.

The excavation started in October 1996 and was finished in March 1997. The excavation team consisted of about forty Bahrainis from the local area, who did a good job in an enjoyable atmosphere. The team was lead by Mustafa Ebrahim, who was assisted by Jaffer Jawad, Ali Jaffer and Ali Juma. Ali Omran executed the field drawings and Saleh Ali took the photographs. The excavation started in the south-eastern quarter with a 5 x 5 m square in the highest part of that quarter in order to get an idea of the stratigraphy of the mound. After another two 5 x 5 m squares were excavated, larger sections from the centre to the edge of the mound where opened. After the south-eastern quarter was excavated, the work continued in the north-eastern part, followed by the south-western and finally the north-western quarters. These areas were all excavated in 5 m trenches from the centre line of the mound to the edge. A 1 m-wide baulk was left in the centre during excavation to illustrate the section.

The excavation revealed a total of ninety-five tombs, ten jar burials and one bathtub-coffin. One of the tombs (no. 16b) dates to the Dilmun period (Bronze Age) and the bathtub-coffin to the late Dilmun period (Iron Age). However, the rest of the burials can safely be placed within the Tylos period. Twenty-six of the tombs showed signs of robbing in antiquity for both objects and building materials, ten graves had been robbed for objects, indicated by small openings in the tombs, and eight tombs for building material, without the grave goods having been disturbed. None of the recorded tombs are believed to have been disturbed in modern times, though bulldozing in the edge of the mound was noticed.

Figure 232. Mound A1-1996-97 before excavation.

Some of the graves produced spectacular findings. The two wooden coffins from Tombs 40 and 44 are unique in their preservation and have added to our knowledge about the wood industry in the region (Andersen *et al.* 2004). Traces of wooden coffins were also recorded from other tombs in this mound. Another very important find was an inscribed stele, which was reused as a capstone for Tomb 44. The inscription is a dedication inscription of a temple made by a Characenian governor in Tylos (Gatier *et al.* 2002).

Grave 47 is one of the richest tombs discovered from the Tylos period in Bahrain. The small burial chamber was covered with a single capstone sealed with mortar. The skeleton had not survived, but the chamber length indicates that the deceased was a child or subadult and the nature of the grave goods suggests that it may have been a girl.

Figure 233. Contour map of Mound A1-1996-97.

Type	No	Trench	Built	Disturbed	Length	Width	Depth	Remarks
Tomb	1	F8	Above bedrock	Yes	221	75	109	Pits in each corner and stepped frame.
Tomb	2	E10			128	71	112	
Tomb	3	F10	Above bedrock		224	70	120	
Tomb	4	E10	Above bedrock		88	40	46	
Tomb	5	G11	On bedrock	Yes	212	56	81	
Tomb	6	F11-F12	On bedrock	Yes	129	70	102	Empty. Impressions of rope in the plaster of the stepped tomb frame at each end. 2 pits in each end of the floor of the tomb.
Tomb	7	G13	On bedrock	Yes	148	57	91	
Tomb	8	F14	On bedrock	Yes	205	65	107	Empty.
Tomb	9	F7	Above bedrock	Yes	60	35	34	Empty. No plaster.
Tomb	10	E5	Above bedrock	Yes	97	42	62	Empty.
Tomb	11	F5	Above bedrock	Yes	70	31	50	
Tomb	12	E6-F7	On bedrock		214	65	92	Pits in each corner and stepped frame.
Tomb	13		Above bedrock	Yes	212	69	99	
Tomb	14	G7	On bedrock		211	66	106	Pits in each corner and stepped frame.
Tomb	15	F7	On bedrock		230	75	97	
Tomb	16b				84	60	51	Dilmun type.
Tomb	16	G5	Above bedrock	Yes	187	58	78	
Tomb	17		Above bedrock		112	44	54	
Tomb	18	E4	Above bedrock	Yes	100	42	14	
Tomb	19	F5	Above bedrock		103	45	53	
Tomb	20	F4	Above bedrock		196	64	100	Stepped frame.
Tomb	21	E4	Above bedrock		107	43	49	
Tomb	22	E4	Above bedrock		95	47	47	
Tomb	23	E3	Above bedrock		204	55	65	
Tomb	24	E3	Above bedrock		84	36	43	
Tomb	25	E3-F3	Above bedrock		204	70	78	
Tomb	26				75	37	45	
Tomb	27				202	50	79	
Tomb	28		Above bedrock		200	59	83	
Tomb	29	G3	Above bedrock	Yes	220	69	85	
Tomb	30		Above bedrock		202	53	86	
Tomb	31		Above bedrock		202	46	72	
Tomb	32	F2	Above bedrock		107	43	49	
Tomb	33			Yes	210	63	60	Empty.
Tomb	34		Above bedrock	Yes	208	65	42	Empty.
Tomb	35	D9	On bedrock		214	65	113	Tomb walls also plastered on the outside.
Tomb	36		On bedrock		211	60	108	
Tomb	37	B8	Above bedrock	Yes	203	67	89	Empty.
Tomb	38	B9	Above bedrock		204	62	88	
Tomb	39	B9	Above bedrock	Yes	212	72	63	
Tomb	40		On bedrock		210	65	124	
Tomb	41		Above bedrock	Yes	198	62	92	Empty.
Tomb	42		Above bedrock	Yes	197	64	87	Empty.
Tomb	43		Above bedrock		201	63	84	
Tomb	44	D12	On bedrock		204	97	103	3 pits across the floor, 1 each end and 1 in the middle.
Tomb	45		On bedrock	Yes	200	65	79	
Tomb	46			Yes	204	63	78	Empty.
Tomb	47	D13	On bedrock		0		78	

Type	No.	BNM No.	Cat. no.	Material	Find type	Number	Remark
Tomb	87	A16351		Stone	N/A	3	
Tomb	87	A16361		Pottery	Weight	2	
Tomb	87	A1075		Silver	Finger ring	1	With gem.
Tomb	87	A10526		Lead	Weight	2	
Tomb	87	N/A		Ivory	Stopper	1	
Tomb	87	A16350		Ivory	Pin head	9	
Tomb	87	A16346		Stone & bronze	Bead	31	
Tomb	87	97-3-240	BO.2	Glazed pottery	Cosmetic pot	1	
Tomb	87	A9066	6.9	Glass	Bottle	1	
Tomb	87			Bronze	N/A	2	
Tomb	87			Bronze	Pin	1	
Tomb	88			Stone & glass	Bead	N/A	
Tomb	88			Bronze	Pin	1	
Tomb	88	N/A		Bone	Ring	1	
Tomb	89			Bronze	Earring	1	
Tomb	89	A16347		Seashell	N/A	3	
Tomb	89	A15982		Stone	Bead	13	
Tomb	90	A10528		Stone	Bead	N/A	
Tomb	90	A10528		Textile	Fragments	N/A	
Tomb	90			Seashell	N/A	2	
Tomb	90			Bronze	Bangle	1	
Tomb	90	A16349		Bronze	Spatula	1	
Tomb	93			Bronze	Finger ring	2	
Tomb	93			Silver	Bracelet	2	
Tomb	93			Stone	Bead	N/A	
Tomb	93	N/A		Wood	Coffin	N/A	Fragments.
Tomb	94	97-3-362	AR.6	Glazed pottery	Bowl	1	
Tomb	94	A16348		Bronze	Bracelet	3	Broken.
Tomb	94			Seashell	N/A	N/A	
Tomb	94			Stone	Bead	N/A	
Tomb	94			Ivory	Fragments	N/A	
Tomb	97	A9710		Ivory	Cosmetic container	1	With stopper.
Tomb	97	A2036		Bronze	Bell	2	
Jar	2			Bronze	Pin	1	Broken.
Jar	2	A14056		Stone	Bead	40	
Jar	2			Seashell	N/A	1	
Jar	2	N/A	AH.1	Glazed pottery	Bowl	1	Broken.
Jar	6			Seashell	N/A	10	
Jar	6			Iron	N/A	N/A	
Jar	6			Silver	Bead	N/A	
Jar	6			Pottery	Bottle	1	
Jar	6	A1825	BX.14	Glazed pottery	Pilgrim flask	1	
Jar	6	A9737		Bronze	Bracelet	1	
Jar	6	97-3-114	BB.4	Glazed pottery	Cup	1	
Fill		97-3-148	BF.51	Glazed pottery	Cup	1	Broken.
Fill		97-3-221	AZ.1	Glazed pottery	Cup	1	Trench D3
Fill				Stone	Stele	1	Trench C9

Table 38. List of finds (Shakhoura Cemetery, Mound A1-1996-97).

Figure 234. Mound A1-1996 97 during excavation.

Figure 235. Section of Mound A1-1996-97.

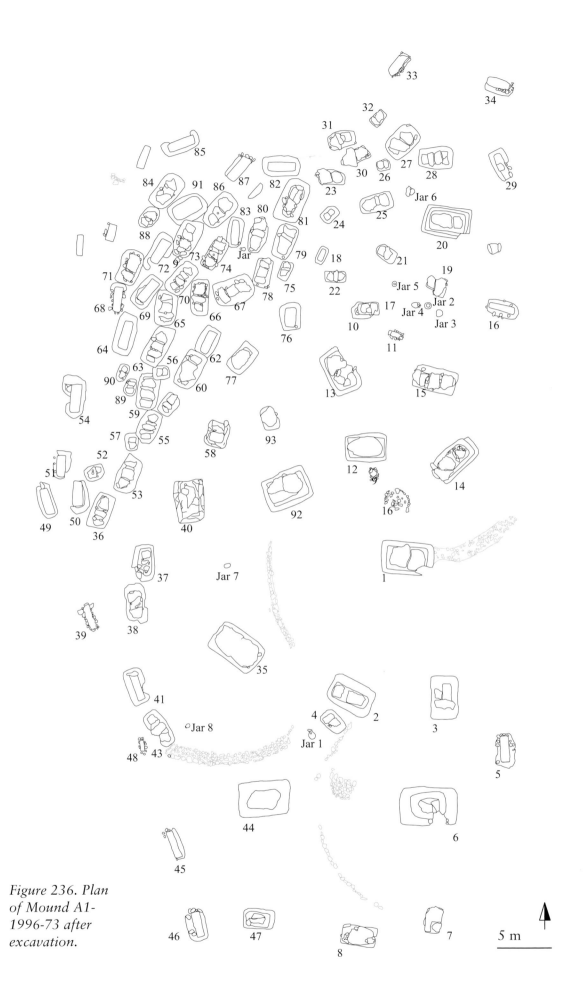

Figure 236. Plan of Mound A1-1996-73 after excavation.

5 m

Figure 237. Mound A1-1996-97, Late Dilmun pot burial (Pot 1).

Figure 238. Tombstone found in the mound fill. Mound A1-1996-97, Trench C 9.

Figure 239. Containers made of ivory from Mound A1-1996-97, Tomb 14 and 97.

Figure 240. Type BA glazed ware cup from Mound A1-1996-97, Tomb 1.

Figure 241. Beads from Mound A1-1996-97, Tomb 2.

123

5 cm

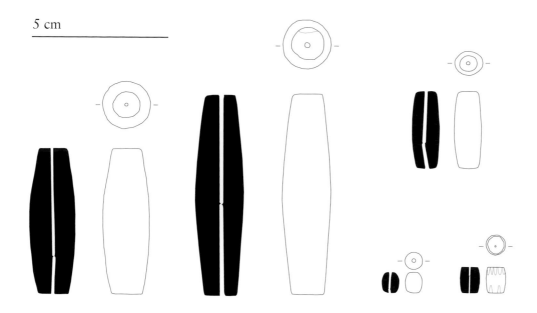

Figure 242. Agate beads from Mound A1-1996-97, Tomb 2.

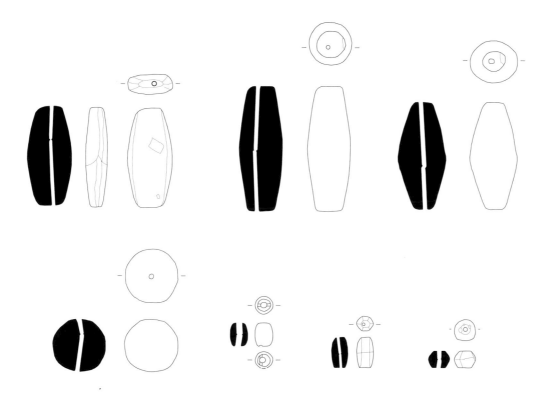

Figure 243. Carnelian beads from Mound A1-1996-97, Tomb 2.

Figure 244. "Pin heads" made of ivory from Mound A1-1996-97, Tomb 2.

5 cm

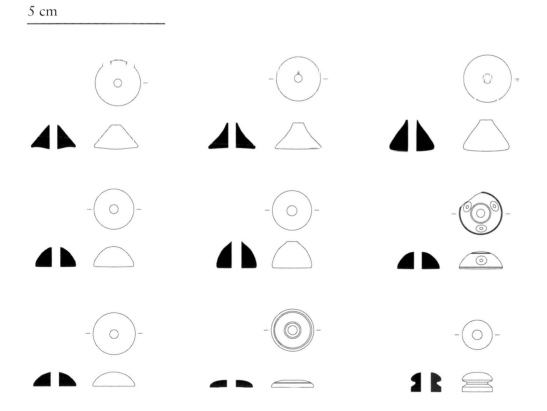

Figure 245. "Pin heads" made of ivory from Mound A1-1996-97, Tomb 2.

Figure 246. Dress pin made of ivory from Mound A1-1996-97, Tomb 2.

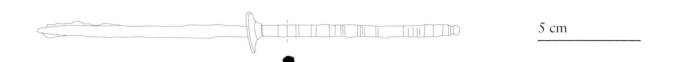

Figure 247. Dress pin made of bronze from Mound A1-1996-97, Tomb 2.

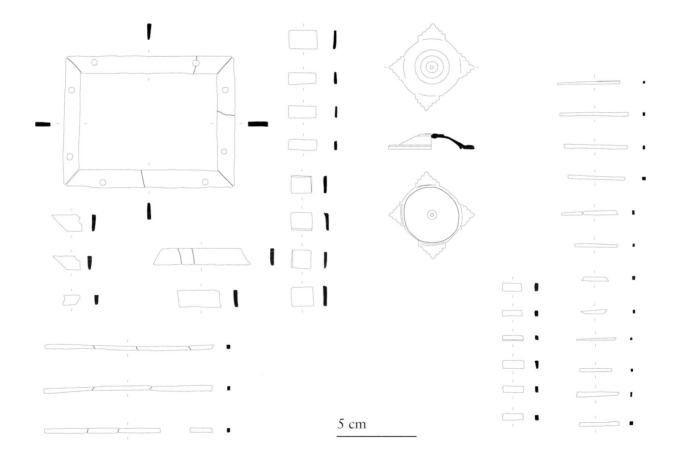

Figure 248. Box inlay made of bone from Mound A1-1996-97, Tomb 2.

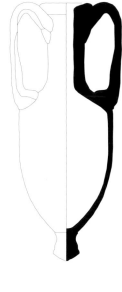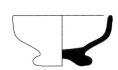

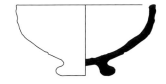

Figure 251. Type BB glazed ware cup from Mound A1-1996-97, Tomb 6.

Figure 252. Type BA glazed ware cup from Mound A1-1996-97, Tomb 7.

Figure 249. Type 1 glass bottle from Mound A1-1996-97, Tomb 2.

Figure 250. Type 1 glass bottle from Mound A1-1996-97, Tomb 2.

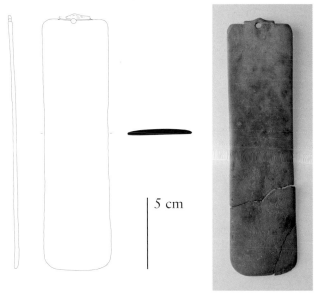

5 cm

Figure 254. Bone "plaque" from Mound A1-1996-97, Tomb 12.

Figure 255. Bone "plaque" from Mound A1-1996-97, Tomb 12.

Figure 253. Mound A1-1996-97, Tomb 12 with trenches in each corner and grave goods.

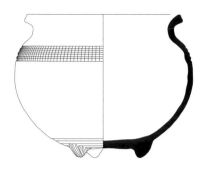

Figure 256. Type AE glazed ware pot from Mound A1-1996-97, Tomb 12.

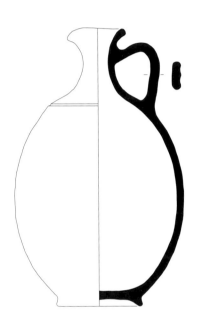

Figure 257. Type BM glazed ware jug from Mound A1-1996-97, Tomb 12.

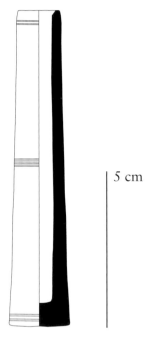

Figure 258. Container made of ivory from Mound A1-1996-97, Tomb 14.

5 cm

Figure 259. Container made of ivory from Mound A1-1996-97, Tomb 14.

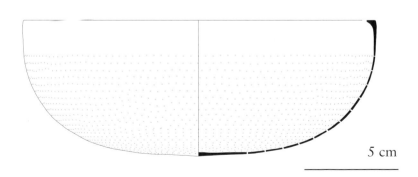

Figure 260. Bronze sieve from Mound A1-1996-97, Tomb 14.

5 cm

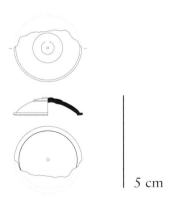

5 cm

Figure 261. Ivory "plate" from Mound A1-1996-97, Tomb 16.

Figure 262. Mound A1-1996-97, Tomb 16b. Dilmun tomb with ring wall.

Figure 263. Type D glazed ware bowl
from Mound A1-1996-97, Tomb 19.

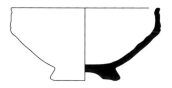

Figure 264. Type BF glazed ware cup
from Mound A1-1996-97, Tomb 20.

Figure 265. Mound A1-1996-97, Tomb 20 with
step frame.

129

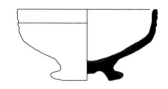

Figure 266. Type AP glazed ware bowl from Mound A1-1996-97, Tomb 28.

Figure 267. Type BA glazed ware cup from Mound A1-1996-97, Tomb 30.

Figure 268. Beads from Mound A1-1996-97, Tomb 32.

Figure 269. Rock crystal bead from Mound A1-1996-97, Tomb 32.

Figure 270. Glass beads from Mound A1-1996-97, Tomb 32.

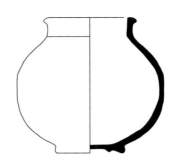

Figure 271. Type AM fine ware unguentarium from Mound A1-1996-97, Tomb 35.

Figure 272. Type AM fine ware unguentarium from Mound A1-1996-97, Tomb 35.

Figure 273. Type BL glazed ware jar from Mound A1-1996-97, Tomb 36.

Figure 274. Type BG glazed ware cup from Mound A1-1996-97, Tomb 36.

Figure 275. Type AQ glazed ware bowl from Mound A1-1996-97, Tomb 36.

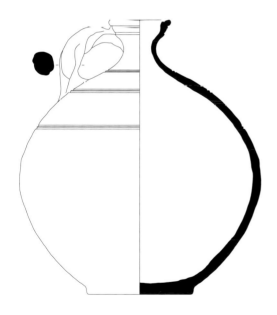

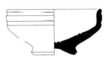

Figure 277. Type BG glazed ware cup from Mound A1-1996-97, Tomb 36.

Figure 276. Non-classified glazed ware jug from Mound A1-1996-97, Tomb 36.

Figure 278. Mound A1-1996-97, Tomb 40 before excavation.

Figure 280. Mound A1-1996-9, Tomb 44 with wooden coffin.

Figure 279. Greek inscription on stone reused as capstone to cover Mound A1-1996-97, Tomb 40.

Figure 281. Mound A1-1996-97, Tomb 47 with grave goods.

Figure 282. Type 1 glass bottle from Mound A1-1996-97, Tomb 47.

Figure 283. Type 3 glass bowl from Mound A1-1996-97, Tomb 47.

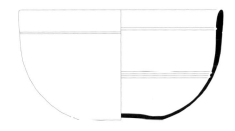

Figure 284. Type 3 glass bowl from Mound A1-1996-97, Tomb 47.

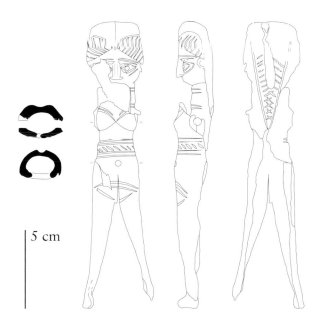

5 cm

Figure 285. Figurine made of bone from Mound A1-1996-97, Tomb 47.

Figure 286. Figurine made of bone from Mound A1-1996-97, Tomb 47.

Figure 287. Bracelet made of folded silver plate from Mound A1-1996-97, Tomb 47.

Figure 288. Type BU glazed ware bottle from Mound A1-1996-97, Tomb 47.

Figure 289. Beads from Mound A1-1996-97, Tomb 56.

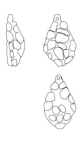

5 cm

Figure 290. Pearl bead from Mound A1-1996-97, Tomb 56.

5 cm

Figure 291. Rock crystal beads from Mound A1-1996-97, Tomb 56.

5 cm

Figure 292. Carnelian beads from Mound A1-1996-97, Tomb 56.

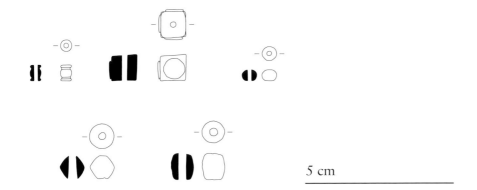

Figure 293. Glass beads from Mound A1-1996-97, Tomb 56.

5 cm

Figure 294. Type BQ glazed ware bottle from Mound A1-1996-97, Tomb 63.

Figure 295. Type BZ glazed ware bottle from Mound A1-1996-97, Tomb 65.

Figure 297. Type CA fine ware bottle from Mound A1-1996-97, Tomb 66.

Figure 298. Type CC plain ware bottle from Mound A1-1996-97, Tomb 65.

Figure 296. Terracotta figurine from Mound A1-1996-97, Tomb 65.

Figure 299. Type BZ glazed ware flask from Mound A1-1996-97, Tomb 65.

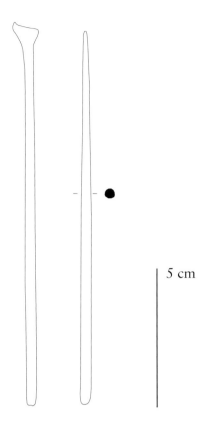

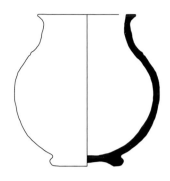

Figure 301. Type BL glazed ware jar from Mound A1-1996-97, Tomb 74.

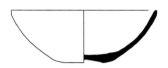

Figure 300. Spatula made of bronze from Mound A1-1996-97, Tomb 71.

Figure 302. Type AQ glazed ware bowl from Mound A1-1996-97, Tomb 74.

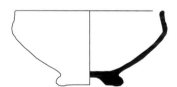

Figure 303. Type BF glazed ware cup from Mound A1-1996-97, Tomb 74.

Figure 304. Type G glazed ware bowl from Mound A1-1996-97, Tomb 75.

Figure 305. Beads from Mound A1-1996-97, Tomb 76.

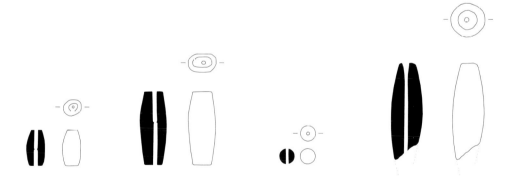

Figure 306. Agate beads from Mound A1-1996-97, Tomb 76.

Figure 308. Ivory bead from Mound A1-1996-97, Tomb 76.

5 cm

Figure 307. Clay bead from Mound A1-1996-97, Tomb 76.

Figure 309. Steatite bead from Mound A1-1996-97, Tomb 76.

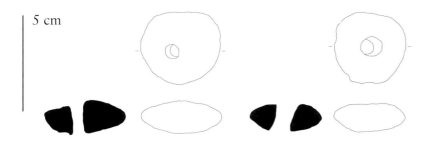

Figure 318. Weights made of clay from Mound A1-1996-97, Tomb 87.

Figure 319. Weights made of clay from Mound A1-1996-97, Tomb 87.

Figure 320. Type 6 glass bottle from Mound A1-1996-97, Tomb 87.

Figure 322. Type BO glazed ware bottle from Mound A1-1996-97, Tomb 87.

Figure 321. Beads from Mound A1-1996-97, Tomb 88.

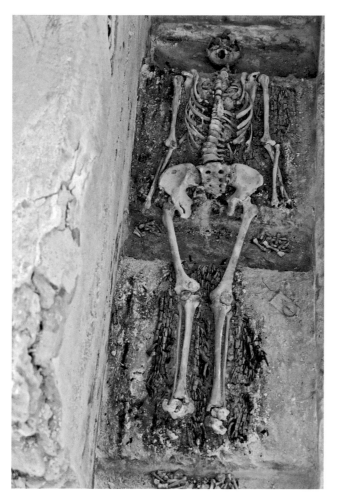

Figure 323. Mound A1-1996-97, Tomb 92 with trenches in the floor and remnants of wood.

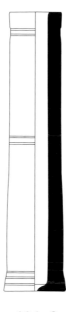

Figure 324. Container made of ivory from Mound A1-1996-97, Tomb 97.

5 cm

Figure 325. Container made of ivory from Mound A1-1996-97, Tomb 97.

5 cm

Figure 326. Bronze bells with iron clappers from Mound A1-1996-97, Tomb 97.

Figure 327. Bronze bells with iron clappers from Mound A1-1996-97, Tomb 97.

Figure 328. Type AZ glazed ware cup from Mound A1-1996-97, Fill Trench D3.

141

Mound 2, 1987
Abbas Ahmed

This mound was located on private land. It measured 12 x 12 m and was circular in shape and flat on the top. The mound was damaged in the southern part, probably due to recent construction nearby.

The excavation was laid out in four quadrants, where Quadrant 1 was in the north-western section, Quadrant 2 in the south-west, Quadrant 3 in the south-east and Quadrant 4 in the north-east. Excavation began on the eastern part of the mound with Quadrants 3 and 4. When this side was completed, the western side was excavated. The excavation continued until bedrock was reached.

Three graves were found. They were orientated in different directions and were built of stone and plastered on the inside and top of each wall.

Type	No	Trench	Built	Disturbed	Length	Width	Depth	Remarks
Tomb	1		On bedrock	·	170	75	70	
Tomb	2		On bedrock		175	65	72	Empty.
Tomb	3		On bedrock	Yes	70	35	15	Empty.

Table 39. List of tombs (Shakhoura Cemetery, Mound 2-1987).

Type	No.	BNM No.	Cat. no.	Material	Find type	Number	Remark
Tomb	1			Bronze	N/A	N/A	
Tomb	1	3600-2-91-6	AQ.72	Glazed pottery	Bowl	1	

Table 40. List of finds (Shakhoura Cemetery, Mound 2-1987).

Mound 2, 1991-92
Abdul Kareem Jassem

Mound 2 was situated in the south-western part of the Shakhoura cemetery. To the north were unexcavated burial mounds, to the west was a garden, to the south was an ancient Islamic settlement, to the east were modern housing and to the south-west was a mosque.

The mound measured 38 m north–south and 23 m east–west and had a height of 1.96 m above the surroundings. Parts of the mound were slightly sunken, especially around the edges, but also in the middle.

For the excavation of the mound, 5 x 5 m trenches were laid out with 1 m-wide baulks left between them. For most of the trenches, the mound fill was removed until bedrock level was reached, whereas for others it was removed until the floor of the mound was reached. After excavation of the trenches was complete, the baulks were removed. The fill of the mound consisted of brown sand and small stones.

The excavation revealed the remains of an Islamic settlement and four tombs and a jar burial from the Tylos period. The Islamic settlement consisted of one room in the south-western corner of the mound. The floor of this room was destroyed, except for a section in the south-eastern corner. Stone and gypsum were used for its construction. Five big storage jars were found in the south-western corner of the room. The room measured 3.7 x 2.7 m and the walls were preserved up to 0.4 m in height.

The four tombs dating to the Tylos period were all built on bedrock. They were rectangular and were orientated in different directions.

Tomb 4 had two steps surrounding the entire chamber. Within the chamber, there were four pits in each corner. The tomb was presumably robbed as the capstones were removed and the chamber was filled with sand. Parts of the tomb walls were also destroyed. Tomb 2 seems to have been used twice as two skeletons were found. One was pushed aside to make room for the second interment.

142

Type	No	Trench	Built	Disturbed	Length	Width	Depth	Remarks
Tomb	1	B2- C2	On bedrock	Yes	213	76	90	
Tomb	2	B3	On bedrock	Yes	200	60	72	
Tomb	3	B3-C3	On bedrock	Yes	190	50	81	
Tomb	4	C4		Yes	230	71	95	4 pits in each corner of floor: east end 20 and 23 cm long, west end 59 and 53 cm long

Table 41. List of tombs (Shakhoura Cemetery, Mound 2-1991-92).

Type	No	Square	Length	Max. Ø	Rim Ø	Remarks
Jar	1	D1				No information.

Table 42. List of burial jars (Shakhoura Cemetery, Mound 2-1991-92).

Type	No.	BNM No.	Cat. no.	Material	Find type	Number	Remark
Tomb	1			Pottery	Fragments		
Tomb	2	3815-2-91-6	BQ.29	Pottery	Jar	1	
Tomb	3			Glazed pottery	Jar	1	
Tomb	3	91-1-13	BO.5	Glazed pottery	Jar	1	
Tomb	3	A9531	6.19	Glass	Bottle	1	
Tomb	3			Ivory	Dress pin head	2	

Table 43. List of finds (Shakhoura Cemetery, Mound 2-1991-92).

Figure 329. Type 6 glass bottle from Mound 2-1991-92, Tomb 3.

Figure 330. Type 6 glass bottle from Mound 2-1991-92, Tomb 3.

Mound 2, 1996-97
Khaleel Al Faraj

The mound was round in shape and had a height of 1.4 m above the surroundings. It was damaged on most sides and was covered with small stones and soft sand.

For the excavation, the mound was divided into four quadrants, with Quadrant 1 to the north-west, Quadrant 2 to the south-west, Quadrant 3 to the south-east and Quadrant 4 to the north-east. No baulks were left between the quadrants. Excavation first began on the eastern side of the mound with Quadrants 3 and 4. When they were excavated, work continued on the western side. The excavation was continued down to the bedrock.

During the excavation, the following finds were discovered in the fill: a circular alabaster vessel, a fragile burial jar and some pottery sherds. Nine tombs were discovered.

Tomb 1, which dates to the Tylos period, was built on bedrock and orientated east–west. It was covered with two capstones and the inside of the walls and floor was plastered with gypsum. The tomb was empty.

143

Type	No	Trench	Built	Disturbed	Length	Width	Depth	Remarks
Tomb	1		On bedrock	Yes	215	125	60	Empty.
Tomb	2		On bedrock	Yes				Empty. Most of walls destroyed. Dilmun type.
Tomb	3		On bedrock	Yes	79	45	27	Empty. Dilmun type.
Tomb	4		On bedrock	Yes				Most of walls destroyed. Dilmun type.
Tomb	5		On bedrock	Yes				Most of walls destroyed and empty. Dilmun type.
Tomb	6		On bedrock	Yes				Most of walls destroyed and empty. Dilmun type.
Tomb	7		On bedrock	Yes				Most of walls destroyed. Dilmun type.
Tomb	8		On bedrock	Yes				Most of walls destroyed and empty. Dilmun type.

Table 44. List of tombs (Shakhoura Cemetery, Mound 2-1996-97).

Type	No.	BNM No.	Cat. no.	Material	Find type	Number	Remark
Tomb	4			Pottery	Jar	1	
Tomb	7			Pottery	Jar	1	
Tomb	7			Pottery	Jar	1	

Table 45. List of finds (Shakhoura Cemetery, Mound 2-1996-97).

Tombs 2–9 date to the Dilmun period and were similar in design. They were all built on bedrock, with one–two or two–three courses of stone, and were partly destroyed, probably by tomb robbers. Since the Dilmun tombs were heavily damaged, they were difficult to measure.

Mound 3, 1991-92
Abdul Kareem Jassem

This mound was located in the western area of Shakhoura and was surrounded by unexcavated burial mounds.

Mound 3 measured 22 m north–south and 16 m east–west and had a height of 0.92 m above the surroundings. The mound was flat on the top and had uneven slopes in the north-eastern part. Small stones and soft sand covered the mound.

Four trenches, which measured 10.5 x 7.5 m, were laid out for the excavation of the mound. Trench 1 was to the north-west, Trench 2 to the south-west, Trench 3 to the south-east and Trench 4 to the north-east. Baulks 1 m wide were left between the trenches during excavation.

Three tombs were found. They were all built on the bedrock. The inside of the tomb chambers were built of cut stone and only the gaps were covered

Type	No.	Trench	Built	Disturbed	Length	Width	Depth	Remarks
Tomb	1	1-4	On bedrock		200	55	50	
Tomb	2	3	On bedrock	Yes	209	95	45	
Tomb	3	3	On bedrock		104	34	37	

Table 46. List of tombs (Shakhoura Cemetery, Mound 3-1991-92).

Type	No.	BNM No.	Cat. no.	Material	Find type	Number	Remark
Tomb	1			Ivory	Dresspin head	1	
Tomb	3	91-1-33	BO.13	Pottery	vessel	1	
Tomb	3	3782-2-91-6	CB.3	Pottery	vessel	1	

Table 47. List of finds (Shakhoura Cemetery, Mound 3-1991-92).

with small stones and gypsum. The inner walls of the tombs were not plastered, as they would normally be.

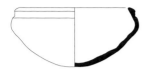

Figure 331. Type CB sand-tempered ware bowl from Mound 3-1991-92, Tomb 3.

Mound 4, 1991-92
Abdul Kareem Jassem

The mound was located on the northern side of Shakhoura village. To the north-east and west of the mound were unexcavated burial mounds, and to the south were houses at some distance.

The mound measured 19 x 22 m and had two elevated parts in the north and south ends with a lower area in between. The height of the northern part was 1.43 m and of the southern part 1.37 m above the surrounding terrain. The mound was covered with small stones and soft sand and had shallow pits scattered all over it.

The mound was excavated in four quadrants. Quadrant 1 in the north-west, Quadrant 2 in the south-west, Quadrant 3 in the south-east and Quadrant 4 in the north-east. Baulks 1 m wide were left between the trenches during excavation. The baulks were excavated when the excavation of the four trenches was finished.

The fill of the mound consisted of brown sand and many small stones. Seven tombs dating to the Tylos period were found. They were orientated in different directions. Most of the tombs were built on the bedrock, and some of them had even been cut into the bedrock. A ring wall was found around Tomb 1, but parts of it on the eastern side were destroyed.

During the excavation, a large burial jar was found. It was fragile and partly damaged. It was apparently used to bury a small child, and had its top covered with a limestone slab and then sealed with gypsum. The height of the jar was 67 cm.

Type	No	Trench	Built	Disturbed	Length	Width	Depth	Remarks
Tomb	1A	3	On bedrock	Yes	185	50	70	Tomb 1B was build on top of Tomb 1A.
Tomb	1B	3			222	75	54	Total depth of the two tombs was 126 cm.
Tomb	2	2	On bedrock	Yes	202	60	60	
Tomb	3	2	On bedrock	Yes	198	50	57	
Tomb	4	2	On bedrock		73	33	25	
Tomb	5	1	On bedrock		203	62	60	Empty.
Tomb	6	4			73	40	33	
Tomb	7	4	On bedrock	Yes	192	48	67	Empty.

Table 48. List of tombs (Shakhoura Cemetery, Mound 4-1991-92).

Type	No	Trench	Length	Max. Ø	Rim Ø	Remarks
Jar	1	2	67			

Table 49. List of burial jars (Shakhoura Cemetery, Mound 4-1991-92).

Type	No.	BNM No.	Cat. no.	Material	Find type	Number	Remark
Tomb	1A	96-1-46	BL.13	Glazed pottery	Vessel	1	Fragmented
Tomb	2	91-1-2	AX.2	Glazed pottery	Vessel	1	
Tomb	4	A12323		Stone/seashell	Bead	N/A	
Tomb	4			Glazed pottery	Vessel	1	Found outside tomb.
Tomb	4			Bronze	Bell	1	
Jar	1			Stone	Bead	N/A	
Jar	1	A9532	13.10	Glass	Bottle	1	

Table 50. List of finds (Shakhoura Cemetery, Mound 4-1991-92).

Some of the graves did not have capstones; they had parts of their walls destroyed and were empty. It is therefore assumed that they were robbed in antiquity. However, Tomb 4 was covered by two capstones, which were sealed with small chips of stone and gypsum. Inside the tomb was the skeleton of a child found together with one glazed bowl and beads of different shapes and sizes.

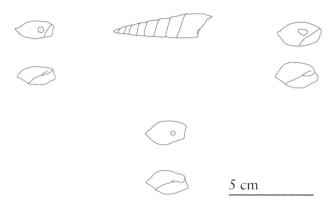

5 cm

Figure 332. Perforated seashells probably used as beads from Mound 4-1991-92, Tomb 4.

Figure 333. Type 13 glass bottle from Shakhoura, Mound 4-1991-92, Jar 1.

Mound 4, 1996-97
Khaleel Al Faraj

To the north of this mound was Mound 5 situated at a distance of 14 m. To the east was a road leading to the nearby village, to the west were unexcavated burial mounds, and to the south was Mound 3 at a distance of 3 m.

The mound measured 16 x 18 m and was almost round. It was 2.75 m high and covered with small stones and soft sand. The mound was damaged from most sides and it had shallow depressions in different parts. For the excavation, the mound was divided into four quadrants and no baulks were left between them.

The mound was built on uneven bedrock. In the mound fill was a clay horse figurine, parts of which were missing. Five tombs were discovered. Tomb 1 was located in the centre of the mound and was the only tomb dating to the Tylos period. Tombs 2–5 were from the Dilmun period.

Mound 5, 1980
Abdul Rahman Sobah

This mound was located between Shakhoura and Magaba. It belonged to a group of mounds in the area, which were surrounded by trees and gardens.

It was evident that most of the mound was robbed and destroyed by farmers from the nearby village before the excavation by the Department was started. These activities had exposed three tombs and they appeared to be the only tombs still left in the

Type	No	Trench	Built	Disturbed	Length	Width	Depth	Remarks
Tomb	1		On bedrock	Yes	260	87	142	Empty.
Tomb	2		On bedrock	Yes	110	62	24	Empty. Dilmun type.
Tomb	3		On bedrock		140	62	42	Dilmun type.
Tomb	4		On bedrock	Yes	158	63	13	Dilmun type.
Tomb	5		On bedrock	Yes	140	62	23	Dilmun type.

Table 51. List of tombs (Shakhoura Cemetery, Mound 4-1996-97).

Type	No.	BNM No.	Cat. no.	Material	Find type	Number	Remark
Tomb	3			Pottery	Jar	1	
Tomb	3			Pottery	N/A	N/A	
Tomb	4			Shell	N/A	N/A	
Fill				Pottery	Horse Figurine	1	

Table 52. List of finds (Shakhoura Cemetery, Mound 4-1996-97).

Type	No	Trench	Built	Disturbed	Length	Width	Depth	Remarks
Tomb	1		On bedrock		191	48	53	
Tomb	2		On bedrock	Yes	132	52	83	
Tomb	3		On bedrock	Yes				Empty.

Table 53. List of tombs (Shakhoura Cemetery, Mound 5-1980).

Type	No.	BNM No.	Cat. no.	Material	Find type	Number	Remark
Tomb	1			Pottery	Bowl	1	
Tomb	2			Pottery	Fragments	N/A	

Table 54. List of tombs (Shakhoura Cemetery, Mound 5-1980).

mound. The excavation focused therefore on these tombs, and due to the poor state of preservation it was completed within a few days.

Mound 5, 1991-92
Abdul Kareem Jassem

Mound 5 was located between Shakhoura village and Abu Saybeh. North of the mound was a road and some houses, to the south and west were some unexcavated burial mounds, and east of the mound were some houses.

Mound 5 measured 17 m north–south and 13 m east–west. It had a height of 1.6 m above the surrounding terrain. A bulldozer had damaged the north-eastern and south-western parts of this mound. This was presumably done to use the mound fill at a nearby construction site. Small stones and soft sand covered the mound.

For the excavation, the mound was divided into two trenches, one covering the northern half, and the other the southern half. A baulk was left between the two trenches. Excavation began in the northern part. The trenches and the baulk were excavated to the bedrock and eight tombs were found.

Tombs 1 and 5 lay in a north–south direction, and Tombs 2, 3, 4, 6, 7 and 8 lay in an east–west direction. There were no capstones on Tombs 1, 6 and 7. Most graves had plastered walls and contained the remains of human skeletons. It appeared that most of them were robbed in antiquity.

Tomb 8 probably dates to the Dilmun period. All the walls of this tomb were missing, but a skeleton was found lying in a foetal position on its right side facing north.

Type	No	Trench	Built	Disturbed	Length	Width	Depth	Remarks
Tomb	1		On bedrock	Yes	195	48	60	
Tomb	2		On bedrock		198	53	70	
Tomb	3		On bedrock		107	43	42	
Tomb	4		On bedrock		191	55	50	
Tomb	5		On bedrock	Yes	60	25	35	Empty.
Tomb	6		On bedrock	Yes	181	40	55	Empty.
Tomb	7		On bedrock	Yes	184	51	65	Empty.
Tomb	8							Dilmun type.

Table 55. List of tombs (Shakhoura Cemetery, Mound 5-1991-92).

Type	No.	BNM No.	Cat. no.	Material	Find type	Number	Remark
Tomb	2			Pottery	Vessel	1	
Tomb	2	A13281		Bronze	Spatula	1	
Tomb	2	3833-2-91-6	AQ.78	Glazed pottery	Vessel	1	

Table 56. List of finds (Shakhoura Cemetery, Mound 5-1991-92).

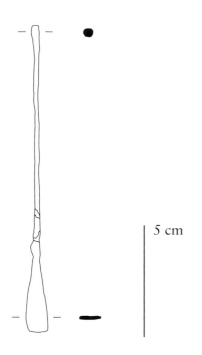

5 cm

Figure 334. Spatula made of bronze Mound 5-1991-92, Tomb 2.

Mound 6, 1991-92
Abdul Kareem Jassem

This mound was located in the north-western part of Shakhoura. To the east was a large unexcavated mound, to the west and south were houses, and to the north was a private garden as well as some houses.

Mound 6 measured 25 m north–south and 22 m east–west. The highest point of the mound was 2.6 m above the surrounding terrain and was located in the northern part of the mound. The mound had an uneven slope to the south and pits around the edges. It was covered with compact sand and small stones.

For the excavation, the mound was divided into four quadrants. Quadrant 1 was to the north-west, Quadrant 2 to the south-west, Quadrant 3 to the south-east and Quadrant 4 to the north-east. Baulks 1 m wide were left between the trenches and only excavated after the quadrants.

Below the mound was a level layer of soft light brown sand. Six tombs and six burial jars were discovered.

Type	No	Trench	Built	Disturbed	Length	Width	Depth	Remarks
Tomb	1		On bedrock		197	66	92	
Tomb	2	4		Yes	215	65	100	
Tomb	3		On bedrock	Yes	194	59	91	
Tomb	4	4	On bedrock		210	52	70	
Tomb	5	3	On bedrock	Yes	224	68	107	
Tomb	6		On bedrock	Yes	217	63	86	

Table 57. List of tombs (Shakhoura Cemetery, Mound 6-1991-92).

Type	No	Square	Length	Max. Ø	Rim Ø	Remarks
Jar	1	1	78	42		Inside covered with bitumen.
Jar	2		78	42		

Table 58. List of burial jars (Shakhoura Cemetery, Mound 6-1991-92).

Type	No.	BNM No.	Cat. no.	Material	Find type	Number	Remark
Tomb	1	126	AF.29	Pottery	Vessel	1	
Tomb	6	125	AF.15	Glazed pottery	Vessel	1	Found outside the tomb.

Table 59. List of finds (Shakhoura Cemetery, Mound 6-1991-92).

All tombs had the inside and upper parts of the walls plastered. They were all were built on bedrock except for Tomb 3, which was built on the layer of soft light brown sand mentioned above. Tombs 1, 3, 4, 5 and 6 contained the remains of human skeletons. The six burial jars were found in various parts of the mound, but information has only been recorded for the first two.

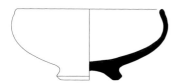

Figure 335. Type AF glazed ware cup from Mound 6-1991-92, Tomb 6.

Mound 7, 1992-93
Dawod Yusuf

Mound 7 was a big mound with a diameter of *c.* 60 m and a height of 2–3.5 m above the surroundings.[8] The surface of the mound was uneven and covered by small stones and soft sand. In the centre was a marked depression measuring 10 x 10 m. This depression is assumed to have been caused by an unrecorded excavation in the past, which may have attempted to find a main chamber. The mound was damaged in several parts because local people had removed sand from the mound.

[8] This mound is referred to as Mound 7-1993 in Volume 1.

Figure 336. Plan of Mound 7-1992-93 after excavation.

Type	No	Trench	Built	Disturbed	Length	Width	Depth	Remarks
Tomb	1	A5		Yes				Empty.
Tomb	2			Yes	220	65	70	Empty.
Tomb	3		On bedrock		220	62	90	
Tomb	4		On bedrock	Yes	120	60	93	Empty.
Tomb	5		On bedrock		220	70	75	
Tomb	6		On bedrock	Yes	210	66	86	South and west wall completely gone.
Tomb	7							Tomb completely destroyed.
Tomb	8	B6	On bedrock		203	68	87	
Tomb	9	B2	On bedrock		207	57	62	
Tomb	10	B8	On bedrock		202	58	52	Empty.
Tomb	11	C2						Some of the southern and eastern walls destroyed.
Tomb	12	C2	On bedrock	Yes	266	72	110	Empty.
Tomb	13	C2	On bedrock	Yes	128	68	112	Empty.
Tomb	14	C2		Yes	70	55	18	Most of the walls destroyed.
Tomb	15	C3	On bedrock	Yes	206	67	92	Empty.
Tomb	16	C3		Yes				Tomb completely destroyed.
Tomb	17		On bedrock		223	51	118	
Tomb	18	C3	Above bedrock		80	41	41	
Tomb	19	C4	On bedrock		225	64	105	Empty.
Tomb	20	C4	On bedrock		206	70	215	Empty.
Tomb	21		On bedrock		224	86	91	The capstone was broken.
Tomb	22	C4	On bedrock		210	70	94	
Tomb	23	C6	On bedrock	Yes	124	61	76	
Tomb	24	C6	On bedrock		220	60	92	Empty.
Tomb	25	C6	On bedrock		215	58	77	
Tomb	26	B5	On bedrock	Yes	224	74	94	Empty chamber.
Tomb	27	B5	On bedrock		224	78	97	Empty chamber.
Tomb	28	B8	On bedrock	Yes	200	61	85	South and west wall completely gone.
Tomb	29	C5	On bedrock		234	68	90	Empty.
Tomb	29A	C7	On bedrock		223	65	90	Empty.
Tomb	30	B7	On bedrock	Yes	209	77	66	
Tomb	31	B7	On bedrock		190	50	63	Empty.
Tomb	32	C8	On bedrock	Yes	202	63	91	
Tomb	33	C8	On bedrock		220	67	85	Empty.
Tomb	34	B9	On bedrock	Yes	202	58	53	Empty.
Tomb	34A	D4	On bedrock	Yes	215	60	90	
Tomb	35	D4	On bedrock	Yes	228	77	116	
Tomb	36	D4	On bedrock	Yes	198	65	105	The capstone was in fragments.
Tomb	37	D5	On bedrock		209	66	85	Empty chamber.
Tomb	38	D5	On bedrock		209	74	87	Empty chamber.
Tomb	39	D5	On bedrock	Yes	190	56	74	Originally three capstones but the one in the middle robbed.
Tomb	40	D2	Above bedrock	Yes	85	40	36	
Tomb	41	D3	On bedrock		220	70	120	
Tomb	42	D3	On bedrock		220	70	110	
Tomb	43	D3	On bedrock		220	68	110	Empty.
Tomb	44	D3	Above bedrock		100	45	58	
Tomb	45	D3	On bedrock	Yes	220	69	93	Originally, three capstones but the one in the middle robbed.
Tomb	46	D6	On bedrock		200	59	80	
Tomb	47	D1	On bedrock	Yes	219	71	77	Empty.
Tomb	48	D2	On bedrock		142	60	73	Empty.
Tomb	49	D2	On bedrock	Yes	209	78	109	Eempty.
Tomb	50	D2		Yes				The walls were completely destroyed.

Type	No	Trench	Built	Disturbed	Length	Width	Depth	Remarks
Tomb	51	D6	On bedrock		220	65	87	Empty.
Tomb	52	D9	On bedrock	Yes	200	75	93	Empty.
Tomb	53	D10	On bedrock	Yes	215	70	110	
Tomb	54	E4	On bedrock	Yes	205	46	75	Originally, four capstones but the one in the middle robbed.
Tomb	55	E4	On bedrock		200	93	97	Originally, three capstones but the one in the east robbed.
Tomb	56	E4	On bedrock		205	60	95	
Tomb	57	E4		Yes	92	61	53	Empty.
Tomb	58	D8	On bedrock		240	70	74	
Tomb	59	d8	On bedrock		225	68	90	
Tomb	60	D8	On bedrock	Yes	223	68	92	Empty.
Tomb	61	D8	On bedrock		210	67	95	
Tomb	62	62	Above bedrock		200	72	97	Originally, four capstones but the one in the west had fallen into the tomb chamber.
Tomb	63		On bedrock	Yes	220	80	112	Empty.
Tomb	64	E3	Above bedrock	Yes	81	64	64	Empty.
Tomb	65	E3		Yes	221	64	95	Empty, and some capstones were robbed.
Tomb	66	E3			225	70	117	
Tomb	67	E5	On bedrock	Yes	220	61	69	
Tomb	68	E5		Yes	221	65	98	Empty.
Tomb	69	E7	On bedrock	Yes	210	56	82	Empty.
Tomb	70	E2	On bedrock	Yes	209	74	119	
Tomb	71	E2	On bedrock		210	59	85	
Tomb	72		On bedrock		214	63	83	
Tomb	73	F7	On bedrock		74	41	45	
Tomb	74	F7	On bedrock		206	60	90	
Tomb	75	E9	On bedrock		214	70	88	
Tomb	76	E8		Yes				The capstones had fallen into the tomb chamber.
Tomb	77	F7	Above bedrock	Yes	101	45	52	Empty.
Tomb	78	F5	Above bedrock		221	70	101	
Tomb	79	F5	Above bedrock		202	71	84	Empty.
Tomb	80	F4	Above bedrock		210	60	75	Empty.
Tomb	81	F4	Above bedrock	Yes	210	78	119	The capstones are lost except 1 in the west.
Tomb	82	F4	Above bedrock	Yes	135	47	62	
Tomb	83	F4						Only a few stones from west wall. In the report there are two tombs numbered 83
Tomb	83	F3	Above bedrock	Yes	80	38	38	In the report, there are two graves numbered 83. Empty.
Tomb	84	F3		Yes	224	72	92	The capstones were broken and had fallen inside. Empty.
Tomb	85	F3	On bedrock	Yes	218	69	119	
Tomb	86			Yes				The tomb was destroyed.
Tomb	87	F3	On bedrock	Yes	223	70	118	Empty.
Tomb	88							No information.
Tomb	89	J4	On bedrock	Yes	214	68	92	
Tomb	90	J5	On bedrock		202	80	100	Originally 4 capstones but the two in the middle had fallen into the tomb. Empty.
Tomb	91	J7	On bedrock	Yes	206	69	92	Some of the capstones were robbed. Empty.
Tomb	92	J5	On bedrock	Yes	224	26	80	Some of the capstones were robbed.
Tomb	93	J5	On bedrock		280	78	96	The capstones were damaged, except for the northern one.
Tomb	94	J4	On bedrock		210	58	75	Empty.
Tomb	95	F4	On bedrock		60	38	47	
Tomb	96	J6			210	65	87	Some capstones were damaged and had fallen into the tomb.

Type	No	Trench	Built	Disturbed	Length	Width	Depth	Remarks
Tomb	97	J6	On bedrock		202	58	74	
Tomb	98			Yes	96	48	59	
Tomb	99	J8	On bedrock		200	74	76	Empty.
Tomb	100	J9	On bedrock		225	64	101	
Tomb	101	J9	Above bedrock		56	56	56	
Tomb	102	E9	On bedrock		226	70	118	Some capstones were robbed and the northern and southern walls destroyed.
Tomb	103	F10	On bedrock	Yes	221	65	110	The capstones were broken. Empty.
Tomb	104	F10	On bedrock	Yes	210	69	77	Empty.
Tomb	105	E10	On bedrock	Yes	215	66	116	
Tomb	106	E10	Above bedrock	Yes	200	80	64	Empty.
Tomb	107	F2	On bedrock	Yes	210	72	108	Empty.
Tomb	108	F8		Yes	86	39	46	The tomb built on the second layer.
Tomb	109	F8	Into bedrock	Yes	237	73	97	Some capstones robbed.
Tomb	110	J7	On bedrock	Yes	224	60	74	2 fragments of the capstones had fallen into the tomb.
Tomb	111	F9	On bedrock	Yes	202	111	70	Empty.
Tomb	112	J8	Above bedrock	Yes	100	44	48	Some capstones robbed. Empty.
Tomb	113		On bedrock		190	75	85	
Tomb	114	F6	On bedrock		225	70	86	
Tomb	115	H5	On bedrock	Yes	235	70	94	Some capstones robbed. Empty.
Tomb	116	H5	On bedrock	Yes	212	69	97	Originally three capstones, but the one in the middle was robbed.
Tomb	117	H5	On bedrock	Yes	219	94	96	Some capstones robbed.
Tomb	118	H7	On bedrock		230	71	96	Empty.
Tomb	119	H7	On bedrock	Yes	214	90	94	
Tomb	120	H7		Yes	69	44	34	The tomb was built on the second layer. Some capstones robbed.
Tomb	121	H7	On bedrock	Yes	200	67	88	Empty.
Tomb	122	H6	On bedrock	Yes	224	73	100	Some capstones robbed.
Tomb	123	H6	On bedrock		422	70	85	Empty.
Tomb	124	H6	On bedrock		230	74	101	Originally, four capstones, but the one to the north was robbed.
Tomb	125	J10	On bedrock	Yes	220	67	110	
Tomb	126	J10	On bedrock	Yes	212	64	65	Empty.
Tomb	127	E11	On bedrock	Yes	207	66	65	Empty.
Tomb	128	H8	On bedrock	Yes	235	76	96	
Tomb	129	H8	On bedrock	Yes	240	85	100	Empty.
Tomb	130		On bedrock	Yes	210	63	100	
Tomb	131	K5	On bedrock		224	75	108	Empty.
Tomb	132	K5	On bedrock	Yes	214	73	110	Empty.
Tomb	133	K5		Yes				Only the floor of the tomb was left.
Tomb	134	K5	On bedrock	Yes	233	70	110	
Tomb	135	K5	On bedrock	Yes	204	64	60	Empty.
Tomb	136	H4	On bedrock	Yes	230	64	62	Empty.
Tomb	137	H4		Yes	210	65	84	
Tomb	138		On bedrock	Yes	213	63	100	Empty.
Tomb	139	K7	On bedrock	Yes	227	69	82	Empty.
Tomb	140		On bedrock	Yes	215	70	90	
Tomb	141	K7	On bedrock		108	43	57	
Tomb	142	K6	On bedrock	Yes	220	72	104	Some capstones robbed.
Tomb	143	K6	On bedrock		215	70	81	
Tomb	144	K4		Yes	227	50	61	

Type	No	Trench	Built	Disturbed	Length	Width	Depth	Remarks
Tomb	145	K4	On bedrock	Yes	193	49	37	Empty.
Tomb	146	K4	On bedrock	Yes	196	52	48	Empty.
Tomb	147	K4	On bedrock	Yes	67	35	40	Most of the eastern walls were destroyed
Tomb	148	K4	On bedrock	Yes	218	55	53	
Tomb	149	K4	On bedrock	Yes	190	48	60	
Tomb	150	K4	On bedrock	Yes	220	46	48	Empty.
Tomb	151	J8	On bedrock		93	43	44	
Tomb	152	F8	On bedrock		208	66	82	Originally, three capstones, but the one in the middle was robbed.

Table 60. List of tombs (Shakhoura Cemetery, Mound 7-1993).

Type	No	Trench	Length	Max. Ø	Rim Ø	Remarks
Jar	1	B5				The jar was damaged.
Jar	2	J8				
Jar	3	J6				
Jar	4	K7	60	55		
Jar	5	K4				
Jar	6	K5				
Jar	7	D8				The jar was damaged.

Table 61. List of jars (Shakhoura Cemetery, Mound 7-1993).

Type	No.	BNM No.	Cat. no.	Material	Find type	Number	Remark
Tomb	3			Bronze	Pin head	1	
Tomb	3			Glazed pottery	Cup	1	Found upside down outside the tomb. Contained ash.
Tomb	5			Bronze	Pin	1	
Tomb	5	12	BF.23	Glazed pottery	Bowl	1	
Tomb	5	13	BA.20	Glazed pottery	Cup	1	Found outside the tomb.
Tomb	8	23	BM.3	Glazed pottery	Jug	1	
Tomb	8	10	AF.10	Glazed pottery	Bowl	1	
Tomb	9	A7665	AC.21	Glazed pottery	Bowl	1	
Tomb	17	19	BA.19	Glazed pottery	Cup	1	Found upside down outside the tomb. Contained ash.
Tomb	17			Bronze	Fragments	N/A	
Tomb	17			Pottery	Fragments	N/A	
Tomb	18	30	BQ.10	Glazed pottery	Bottle	1	
Tomb	19			Glazed pottery	Cup	1	Found upside down outside the tomb. Contained ash.
Tomb	21	33	AF.5	Glazed pottery	Cup	1	Found upside down outside the tomb. Contained ash.
Tomb	22	69	BU.15	Glazed pottery	Bottle	1	
Tomb	24	18	AH.37	Glazed pottery	Cup	1	Found outside the tomb. Contained ash.
Tomb	25	1	AD.10	Glazed pottery	Cup	1	Found outside the tomb. Contained ash.
Tomb	25	N/A	AC.14	Glazed pottery	Bowl	1	
Tomb	26	3	BF.16	Glazed pottery	Cup	1	Found upside down outside the tomb. Contained ash.
Tomb	27	2	BH.4	Glazed pottery	Cup	1	Found upside down outside the tomb. Contained ash.
Tomb	29A	2	CX.7	Pottery	Cup	1	
Tomb	30			Iron	Fragments	1	
Tomb	30	6	BF.60	Glazed pottery	Bowl	1	
Tomb	30			Iron	N/A	1	
Tomb	30			Glazed pottery	Jug	1	

Type	No.	BNM No.	Cat. no.	Material	Find type	Number	Remark
Tomb	30	7	AE.28	Glazed pottery	Vessel	1	
Tomb	30	5	AC.20	Glazed pottery	Bowl	1	
Tomb	30			Gold	Earring	1	
Tomb	32	47	AC.68	Glazed pottery	Bowl	1	
Tomb	32			Stone	Bead	26	
Tomb	32			Bronze	Pin	1	
Tomb	32			Iron	Finger ring	1	
Tomb	32			Ivory	Pin head	2	
Tomb	33	15	AH.25	Glazed pottery	Cup	1	Found upside down outside the tomb. Contained ash.
Tomb	34A	11	BF.73	Glazed pottery	Cup	1	Found outside the tomb.
Tomb	35	16	BF.59	Glazed pottery	Cup	1	Found upside down outside the tomb. Contained ash.
Tomb	36	72	BG.8	Glazed pottery	Cup	1	Found upside down outside the tomb. Contained ash.
Tomb	37	37	AH.22	Glazed pottery	Cup	1	Found upside down outside the tomb. Contained ash.
Tomb	38	76	BA.17	Glazed pottery	Cup	1	Found upside down outside the tomb. Contained ash.
Tomb	40			Stone	Bead	1	
Tomb	41			Pottery	Jar	4	
Tomb	42	4	BF.44	Glazed pottery	Cup	1	Found upside down outside the tomb. Contained ash.
Tomb	44			Bronze	Spindle	1	
Tomb	44			Stone	Bead	N/A	
Tomb	44	168	AT.4	Glazed pottery	Bowl	1	
Tomb	45			Glazed pottery	Jar	1	
Tomb	45			Glazed pottery	Bowl	1	
Tomb	45			Seashell	N/A	1	
Tomb	45			Ivory	N/A	1	
Tomb	46	20	AH.3	Glazed pottery	Cup	1	Found upside down outside the tomb. Contained ash.
Tomb	46	32	AE.11	Glazed pottery	Vessel	1	
Tomb	46	31	AC.17	Glazed pottery	Bowl	1	
Tomb	51			Glazed pottery	Cup	1	Found outside the tomb.
Tomb	53			Bronze	Fragments	N/A	
Tomb	56	73	AQ.10	Glazed pottery	Bowl	1	
Tomb	58	17	AH.26	Glazed pottery	Cup	1	Found upside down outside the tomb. Contained ash.
Tomb	58	24	AE.29	Glazed pottery	Vessel	1	
Tomb	58	25	AC.71	Glazed pottery	Bowl	1	
Tomb	59	31	BA.12	Glazed pottery	Cup	1	Found upside down outside the tomb. Contained ash.
Tomb	59	153	AC.19	Glazed pottery	Bowl	1	
Tomb	61	29	E.1	Glazed pottery	Bowl	1	
Tomb	61	28	AC.63	Glazed pottery	Bowl	1	
Tomb	61	27	K.7	Glazed pottery	Bottle	1	
Tomb	61			Ivory	Pin head	5	
Tomb	61			Stone	Pin head	3	

Type	No.	BNM No.	Cat. no.	Material	Find type	Number	Remark
Tomb	61			Stone	Bowl	1	
Tomb	61			Stone	Bead	17	
Tomb	61			Bronze	Spindle	1	
Tomb	61			Ivory	Pin head	1	
Tomb	61			Ivory	Bowl	1	
Tomb	61			Alabaster	Bowl	1	
Tomb	61			Seashell	N/A	1	
Tomb	61			Gold	Mouth band	1	
Tomb	62			Glazed pottery	Cup	1	Found upside down outside the tomb. Contained ash.
Tomb	62	122	AC.58	Glazed pottery	Bowl	1	
Tomb	62	123	BM.5	Glazed pottery	Jug	1	
Tomb	62	A228	AE.35	Glazed pottery	Vessel	1	
Tomb	67	115	BA.18	Glazed pottery	Cup	1	Found outside the tomb.
Tomb	70	26	BE.56	Glazed pottery	Cup	1	Found upside down outside the tomb. Contained ash.
Tomb	70			Pottery	Bowl	1	
Tomb	70			Bronze	Fragments	N/A	
Tomb	72	38	AH.44	Glazed pottery	Cup	1	Found upside down outside the tomb. Contained ash.
Tomb	73			Stone	Bead	21	
Tomb	73			Seashell	N/A	1	
Tomb	74	34	AF.30	Glazed pottery	Cup	1	Found upside down outside the tomb.
Tomb	75	133	CS.12	Glazed pottery	Vessel	1	
Tomb	75	36	AH.31	Glazed pottery	Cup	1	Found upside down outside the tomb. Contained ash.
Tomb	77	35	AH.16	Glazed pottery	Cup	1	Found upside down outside the tomb.
Tomb	78	107	BL.20	Pottery	Jar	1	
Tomb	79	119	AF.7	Glazed pottery	Cup	1	Found upside down outside the tomb. Contained ash.
Tomb	80	41	BF.54	Glazed pottery	Cup	1	Found outside the tomb.
Tomb	82	118	DB.12	Glazed pottery	Bottle	1	
Tomb	82			Pottery	Jar	1	
Tomb	82	A8929	6.1	Glass	Bottle	1	
Tomb	82			Stone	Bead	N/A	
Tomb	82			Bronze	Earring	2	
Tomb	85			Pottery	Bowl	1	
Tomb	90	40	AF.8	Glazed pottery	Cup	1	Found upside down outside the tomb. Contained ash.
Tomb	93			Pottery	Bottle	1	
Tomb	93			Bronze	N/A	1	
Tomb	95	186	BQ.6	Glazed pottery	Bottle	1	
Tomb	95			Bronze	Pin	1	
Tomb	95			Bronze	Dummy	1	
Tomb	100	A7491	BE.71	Glazed pottery	Cup	1	Found outside the tomb.
Tomb	101			Bronze	Pin	1	
Tomb	101			Iron	N/A	1	
Tomb	101			Stone	Bead	N/A	
Tomb	101	161	AT.7	Glazed pottery	Bowl	1	
Tomb	101			Seashell	N/A	1	
Tomb	102			Bronze	N/A	1	
Tomb	102			Ivory	Pin head	1	
Tomb	105	108	AQ.22	Glazed pottery	Bowl	1	
Tomb	108			Glazed pottery	Vessel	1	

Type	No.	BNM No.	Cat. no.	Material	Find type	Number	Remark
Tomb	108			Seashell	N/A	1	
Tomb	108			Glazed pottery	Bottle	1	
Tomb	108			Stone	Bead	N/A	
Tomb	108			N/A	Finger ring	1	
Tomb	109			Glazed pottery	Cup	1	Found outside the tomb.
Tomb	110	169	AH.24	Glazed pottery	Cup	1	Found upside down outside the tomb. Contained ash.
Tomb	113	136	AH.11	Glazed pottery	Cup	1	Found upside down outside the tomb. Contained ash.
Tomb	114	N/A	AH.41	Glazed pottery	Cup	1	Found outside the tomb.
Tomb	114	157	AE.20	Glazed pottery	Vessel	1	
Tomb	114	156	AC.27	Glazed pottery	Bowl	1	
Tomb	114	A10633		Bronze	Bowl	1	
Tomb	114			Bronze	Fragments	N/A	
Tomb	116	167	AF.3	Glazed pottery	Cup	1	Found upside down outside the tomb. Contained ash.
Tomb	119			Stone	Bead	N/A	
Tomb	123			Glazed pottery	Cup	1	Found outside the tomb.
Tomb	125			Stone	Bead	1	
Tomb	125			N/A	Finger ring	1	
Tomb	125			Pottery	Vessel	1	
Tomb	128			Pottery	Bowl	1	
Tomb	128			Bronze	Fragments	N/A	
Tomb	131	162	BF.56	Glazed pottery	Cup	1	Found upside down outside the tomb. Contained ash.
Tomb	137			Glazed pottery	Bowl	1	
Tomb	143			Bronze	Fragments	N/A	
Tomb	143	160	BR.3	Glazed pottery	Bottle	1	Found outside the tomb. Covered by shells.
Tomb	149			Glazed pottery	Bowl	1	
Tomb	151			Bronze	Bracelet	2	
Tomb	151			Bronze	Bead	1	
Tomb	151	106	NON.10	Glazed pottery	Bowl	1	
Tomb	151			Stone	Bead	7	
Jar	4	A7653	BG.9	Pottery	Cup	1	
Jar	4			N/A	N/A	1	
Jar	4			Stone	Bead	1	
Jar	4			Seashell	N/A	1	

Table 62. List of finds (Shakhoura Cemetery, Mound 7-1993).

The excavation of the mound was conducted in trenches measuring 5x5 m with 1 m-wide baulks in between. All trenches were excavated until bedrock or virgin soil. A total of 152 tombs from the Tylos period were found. They were orientated in different directions with Tomb no. 114 in the centre. The tombs appear to have been built on two levels. On the lower level, the tombs were built on bedrock, and on the upper level, they were built on the ancient surface or in the mound fill. Most tombs were robbed, as parts of the capstones and chamber walls had been damaged in order to enter the tomb. All the graves had plastered walls and were covered by capstones made either of limestone or beach rock (*farush*). In addition to the tombs were seven burial jars.

The 152 graves contained a wide variety of grave goods, e.g. glazed pottery, stone beads, bronze spindles, gold mouth bands, ivory and stone dress pins, alabaster bowls, bronze and gold earrings, and iron finger rings. Many of the glazed pottery vessels were found turned upside down on top of the capstone or along the edges and some of them contained ashes.

Tomb 61 was especially rich in the quantity of grave goods. The tomb was in very good condition with the capstones well sealed with small stones and gypsum. It was observed, however, that although this tomb was clearly undisturbed, it did not contain a skeleton.

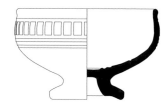

Figure 337. Type BA glazed ware cup from Mound 7-1992-93, Tomb 5.

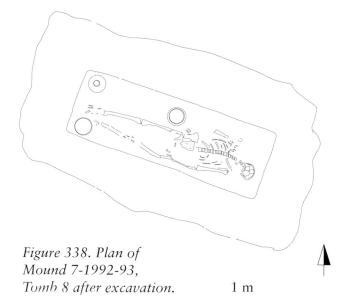

Figure 338. Plan of Mound 7-1992-93, Tomb 8 after excavation.

1 m

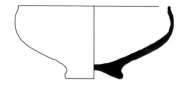

Figure 339. Type AC glazed ware bowl from Mound 7-1992-93, Tomb 9.

Figure 340. Type AF glazed ware cup from Mound 7-1992-93, Tomb 21.

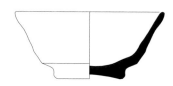

Figure 341. Type AH glazed ware cup from Mound 7-1992-93, Tomb 24.

Figure 342. Type AD glazed ware bowl from Mound 7-1992-93, Tomb 25.

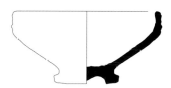

Figure 343. Type AC glazed ware bowl from Mound 7-1992-93, Tomb 25.

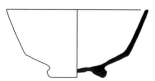

Figure 344. Type BF glazed ware cup from Mound 7-1992-93, Tomb 26.

Figure 345. Type BH glazed ware bowl from Mound 7-1992-93, Tomb 27.

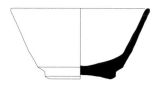

Figure 346. Type AH glazed ware cup from Mound 7-1992-93, Tomb 33.

Figure 350. Type AC glazed ware bowl from Mound 7-1992-93, Tomb 58.

Figure 347. Type BF glazed ware cup from Mound 7-1992-93, Tomb 35.

Figure 351. Type E glazed ware bowl from Mound 7-1992-93, Tomb 61.

Figure 348. Type AT glazed ware bowl from Mound 7-1992-93, Tomb 44.

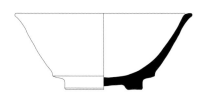

Figure 352. Type AH glazed ware cup from, Mound 7-1992-93, Tomb 72.

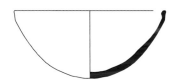

Figure 353. Type CS glazed ware bowl from Mound 7-1992-93, Tomb 75.

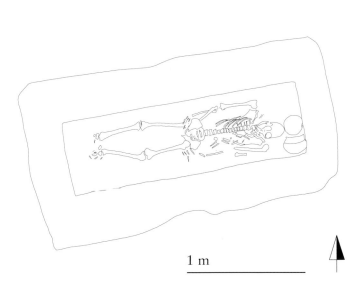

1 m

Figure 349. Plan of Mound 7-1992-93, Tomb 46 after excavation.

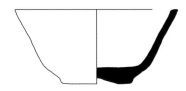

Figure 354. Type AH glazed ware cup from Mound 7-1992-93, Tomb 77.

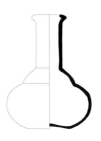

Figure 355. Type 6 glass bottle from Mound 7-1992-93, Tomb 82.

Figure 356. Type 6 glass bottle from Mound 7-1992-93, Tomb 82.

Figure 359. Type AT glazed ware bowl from Mound 7-1992-93, Tomb 101.

Figure 360. Type AQ glazed ware bowl from Mound 7-1992-93, Tomb 105.

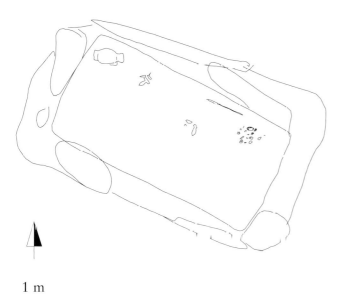

1 m

Figure 357. Plan of Mound 7-1992-93, Tomb 95 after excavation.

1 m

Figure 361. Plan of Mound 7-1992-93, Tomb 108 after excavation.

Figure 358. Type BE glazed ware cup from Mound 7-1992-93, Tomb 100.

Figure 362. Type AC glazed ware bowl from Mound 7-1992-93, Tomb 114.

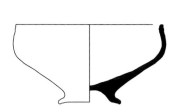

Figure 363. Type BF glazed ware cup from
Mound 7-1992-93, Tomb 131.

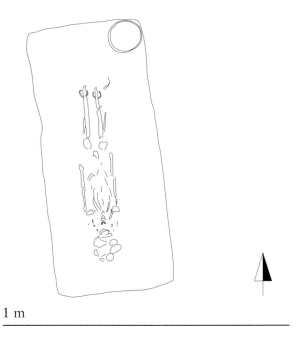

1 m

Figure 364. Plan of Mound 7-1992-93, Tomb 151
after excavation.

1 m

Figure 365. Plan of Mound 7-1992-93, Tomb 175
after excavation.

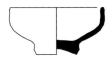

Figure 366. Type BG glazed ware cup from
Mound 7-1992-93, Jar 49.

The chronological development

Søren Fredslund Andersen

4

In Volume 1, the glass and pottery vessels were analysed, resulting in the definitions of five distinctive chronological phases and in the previous chapters a large corpus of tombs and assemblages of grave goods was presented. It is the aim of this chapter to examine continuity and changes in burial practices during the Tylos period by looking at the development of mounds, tomb architecture, tombstones and choice of grave goods.

The discussions are based on the material presented in the previous chapters, supplemented by already published data and selected data from other Bahraini excavations.[9] The excavations presented in Chapters 2 and 3 lack recordings of observations of stratigraphical relations between the different

tombs within a mound. In the absence of such observations that could have led to an intra-site sequence, the dating of tomb assemblages has to rely exclusively on the presence of datable material in the tomb, i.e. pottery and glass vessels, which limits the possibilities for further analyses in a chronological perspective, since only tombs with grave goods can be included.

The burial mounds and tomb architecture

Taking a closer look at the cemeteries, we can observe a common pattern in the development of the mounds in many cases. In Phases I and II the tombs were built as rectangular cists just slightly bigger than the deceased and they seem to have been cov-

Figure 369. Tombs, Shakhoura Mound 1-1992-93.

[9] Relevant unpublished data is listed in Appendix 1.

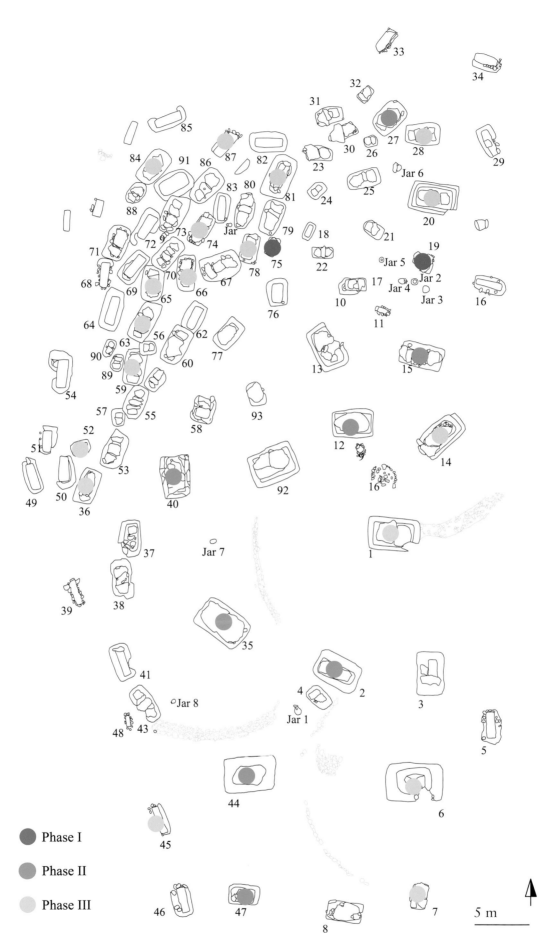

Figure 370. Plan of Shakhoura Mound A1-1996-97 with datable tombs marked. Tomb 1, 6, 7, 14 and 20 are dated to Phase III, but the vessels dating these tombs are also attested in Phase II contexts (Type BA, BB and BF).

Phase I

Phase II

Phase III

5 m

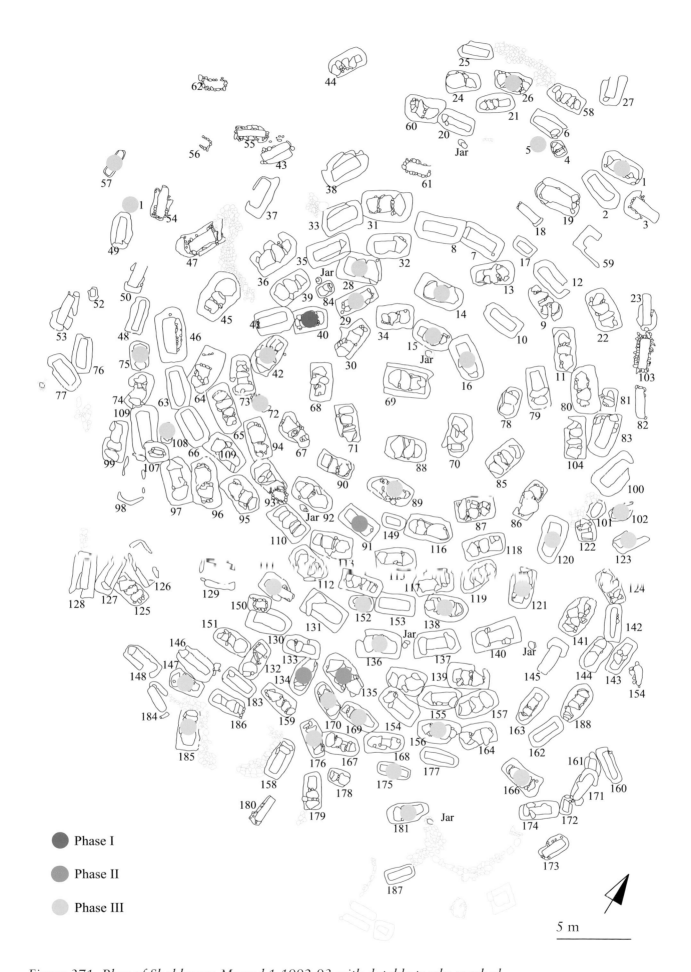

Figure 371. Plan of Shakhoura Mound 1-1992-93 with datable tombs marked.

Phase I

Phase II

Phase III

5 m

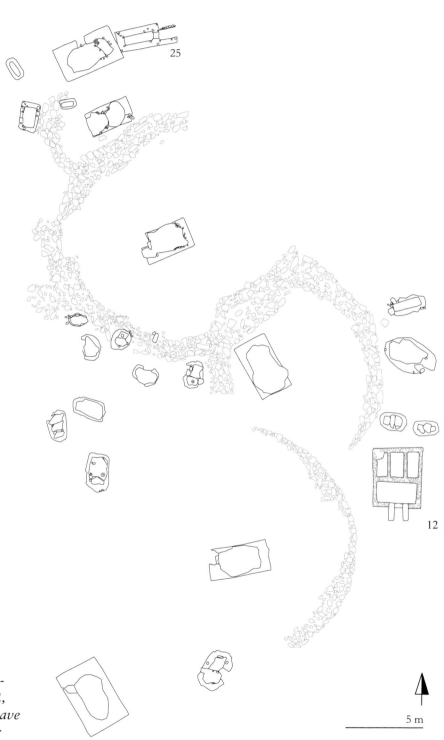
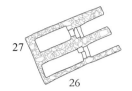

Figure 372. Plan of Saar Mound 1-1991-92, where Tombs 12, 25, 26 and 27 may have been constructed for multiple interments.

5 m

Figure 373. Multi-chambered tombs on top of ordinary tombs. Shakhoura, Mound B2-2003.

Figure 374. View into multi-chambered tombs. Shakhoura, Mound B2-2003.

ered by individual mounds. Good examples of such early burials were found during the Danish excavations, of a group of five small mounds in an pylon T158 in the al-Maqsha area. Only one of the dated tombs (Mound 5, Tomb 985.EH) seems to date later than Phase I (Jensen 2003, but with revised datings). The earliest phase of Shakhoura Mound A1 1996-97 dates to Phase II and a similar pattern of individual mounds can be seen in the south-eastern quarter of this mound (Figure 370). It would also appear that the tombs dating to the earlier phases are orientated approximately east–west.

During Phase II, the individual mounds start to coalesce and in Phase III new tombs were clearly placed at the edge of already existing mounds (Figure 370 and Figure 371). The tombs are no longer orientated in any specific direction, but seem to be tangent to the edge of the existing mound. The tomb architecture is, however, still as it was in the earlier periods, i.e. a built-up and plastered cist (Figure 369).

In Phase IV the simple cists were still used for burials, but multi-chambered tombs seem to have been introduced. Often evidence of such tombs was found at the edge of mounds (Figure 372 and Figure 373) but due to their exposed position, they have

often suffered badly from the decay of the protecting mound and from stone robbing for building material in later periods. This has also affected the possibilities of recovering complete or almost complete vessels that could serve as independent dating evidence. However, the position of the multi-chambered tombs on the periphery of the mound and the increased reuse of tombs (see below) strongly indicate that multi-chambered tombs date to Phase IV or Phase V.

Tombstones

An interesting group of anthropomorphic tombstones and tombstones with reliefs depicting a human in frontal pose, has been found. They are made of local oolitic limestone and are between 16 and 80 cm high. Very often, the tombstones were found in the mound fill and their specific relation to tombs cannot be reconstructed on the basis of the available documentation. A large group of tombstones was found in a garden near Qala'at al-Bahrain apparently out of their original context (Lombard 1999: 204), but in a few occasions, we have the original setting.

One and a half metres west of a tomb in Saar, most likely dating to Phase I or II on the basis of a

Figure 375. Group of tombstones at the edge of Shakhoura Mound 1-1992-93, Trench J3.

bowl with angular profile in grey ware, were three tombstones of the simple anthropomorphic type (see below) (Jensen 2003: 150–153, Grave 962).

Two tombstones are inscribed in Greek. They are also both of the simple anthropomorphic type and the inscriptions give the names and patronymics of the deceased, and the names are Semitic. One inscription also provides the year and probably the ethnic origin of the deceased, as line three could be read "of Alexandria". However, that line is very worn and the reading insecure. The year was 195 and most likely in the Seleucid era, giving a date of 118/117 BC (Gatier, Lombard & al-Sindi 2002: 226–229) and thus within Phase I. The other inscription states that the deceased was a captain (2002: 229). Although the evidence is limited, it would appear that the association of tombstones with a single tomb is a phenomenon relating to Phases I to II.

Later the tombstones appear in some cases to have been placed in groups at the periphery of the mound and it is unclear if they were associated with a specific tomb or with the cemetery in general. Examples of such groups are known from Shakhoura Mound 1-1992-93 (Figure 375) and from al-Maqsha (Abdul Kareem Jassem, personal communication 2003 and 2004).

Stylistically three main groups of anthropomorphic tombstones can be identified, with some exceptions (e.g. Lombard 1999: no. 360). A rather simple form characterizes the first group. They most often have a rectangular body with concave sides and a round or oval piece on top forming a head (e.g. Figure 149). The two tombstones with an inscription were of this type. A variant has a rendering of anatomical details of the face (e.g. Figure 163, Lombard 1999: no. 353). Related tombstones have been found in Yemen in funeral contexts tentatively dated to the third to second century BC (Vogt 2002: nos 265 & 267) and in Phoenicia related pieces have been reported from Lebanon (Sader 2005: nos 9 and 50). Further away, closely related tombstones are also known from Chersonesos on the Crimean peninsula (Ivanova, Cubova & Kolesnikova 1976: nos 113–118) where the type has been dated to the fourth to second century BC and traditionally taken as evidence of Hellenistic influence (Kolesnikova 1977), although this is currently debated (V. Stolba, personal communication 2005).

The second type illustrates a person clad in a *tunica* with a *himation* and a veil over the head, which is held in place by the right elbow (Lombard 1999: nos 355 & 357). In Palmyrene tomb reliefs, females

172

Figure 376. Tombstone with relief.

dering of the faces of a few of the Phoenician type tombstones illustrates great similarities with late Parthian sculpture, whereas others seem stylistically to rely on earlier East Mediterranean prototypes. It is likely that the type was introduced in Phase II or III. Stylistically and iconographically, the different types of tombstones find parallels in a very wide area, since tombstones related to the Bahraini ones are attested in the Hellenistic and early imperial period on the Crimean peninsula, Carthage, Lebanon, Syria and Yemen (see above).

Skeletal remains

The skeletal remains from a large number of tombs have been analysed, but only eighty-two of these tombs can be dated by their content. This information provides an indication of the number of burials in each chamber in the different periods.

	I	II	III	IV
Collective	0	4	12	9
Single	15	9	33	0
Total	15	13	45	9

Table 67. Number of tombs with single or collective burials in each phase.

	I	II	III	IV
Collective	0%	31%	27%	100%
Single	100%	69%	73%	0%

Table 68. Frequencies of tombs with single or collective burials in each phase.

are very often depicted clad in a similar way, although the rendering is more detailed (e.g. Dentzer-Feydy & Teixidor 1993: nos 162 & 174). Related reliefs are also known from Chersonesos (Ivanova, Cubova & Kolesnikova 1976: nos 152 & 155).

A large group illustrates a male figure in frontal pose, with his right arm raised with the palm forward and the left hand holding the drapery (Figure 376). The rendering of a few of the faces is closely related to late Parthian sculpture (see Lombard 1999: no. 361), but the iconography does not find exact parallels in Mesopotamia. However, exact parallels are common in Phoenician cemeteries both in the eastern Mediterranean region (e.g. Louvre inv. no. AO 29410 from Syria), and in the western colonies, for example at Carthage in the centuries before the beginning of our era (Moscati 2001: 367).

Independent dating of the tombstones is problematic. A few of the simple anthropomorphic tombstones can be dated according to their contextual relation with a dated tomb, and one tombstone was inscribed with a date in the Seleucid era. This type appears, therefore, to date to Phases I and II, which corresponds well with the predominantly Hellenistic dating of the widely distributed parallels. The ren-

From Table 67 and Table 68 it can be observed that a gradual change from individual to collective burials takes place from Phases I to IV, which corresponds well with the development of the tomb architecture from individual monuments to tombs built for multiple interments (see above in this chapter). The similarity between the figures for Phases II and III is probably because these phases are relatively short and no significant development in the attitude towards burials took place.

The grave goods

During analysis of the pottery and glass vessels in Volume 1 it was documented that small toilet bottles and containers became more frequent from Phases I to IV compared with vessels related to drinking and eating. In Phase I there was a preference for vessels related to eating. In Phases II and III vessels related to drinking became more frequent and in Phases IV and V the vessels associated with personal adornment were most frequent. This cannot be explained by technical innovations only, but could indicate that perfume and other substances became a preferred choice as grave goods. This may be a result of closer relations with the west, where perfumed oils and make-up had a long and strong tradition. However, the changes could also illustrate a change of function for the grave goods. The vessels associated with eating could be understood as containers for provision for the journey to the underworld. Drinking is more of a social event and the drinking vessels placed in the tombs in Phases II and III could have been needed for participating in the afterlife banquet. In the final phases the self-representation of the deceased may have become the most significant factor for choosing grave goods, since vessels that can be related to personal adornment were preferred. This suggests a gradual change in the social attitude towards burials.

Pottery and glass vessels were not the only grave goods, and it is therefore possible to look at the frequencies of other grave goods according to the categories described in the introduction in a chronological perspective. Most of the other finds were probably intended for personal adornment, but a few categories may have had a symbolic value in relation to the funeral ceremony. Since the only possibility for dating tomb assemblages is on their content of glass and pottery vessels, such vessels will therefore be present in every assemblage in the sample analysed below. The tableware and perfume container groups, which consist mainly of glass and pottery vessels, will therefore be over-represented and must be excluded. There are, however, no indications that the presence of other find groups is contingent upon the presence of tableware or perfume containers, so the picture presented below should provide an unbiased view. A total of 931 tombs were recorded, of which 511 contained grave goods and 307 could be dated. Since a tomb can contain different categories of grave goods, the total number of tombs in each phase is the number of dated tombs with grave goods.

Category/Phase	I	II	III	IV
Bead	16	21	70	3
Coin	0	4	13	1
Misc.	1	8	20	0
Food	8	1	3	0
Jewellery	11	18	31	6
Pins	11	29	73	8
Shell	4	7	24	3
Stone	1	2	5	3
Tool	0	0	18	1
No. of dated tombs	26	70	200	11

Table 69. Number of dated tombs containing certain categories of grave goods.

Category/Phase	I	II	III	IV
Bead	62%	30%	35%	27%
Coin	0%	6%	7%	9%
Misc.	4%	11%	10%	0%
Food	31%	1%	2%	0%
Jewellery	42%	26%	16%	55%
Pins	42%	41%	37%	73%
Shell	15%	10%	12%	27%
Stone	4%	3%	3%	27%
Tool	0%	0%	9%	9%

Table 70. Frequency of dated tombs containing certain categories of grave goods.

From Table 70 it can be observed that the frequency of most categories of grave goods is relatively stable during the four phases. Glass and stone beads are common and so is a wide range of jewellery. Kohl-sticks, pins or spindles are also often found, whereas tools of various kinds occur only in very low numbers. The number of dated tombs in Phases I and IV are limited and due to the development from individual to collective burials the figures are not comparable. With the data available, it is therefore not possible to verify the hypothesis brought forward in Volume 1.

Social segmentation

Søren Fredslund Andersen

5

Sometimes, but not always, the burials reflect the status of the deceased in life and it is the aim of this chapter to shed some light on the social organization of Tylos period society as indicated by the burial data.[10]

In Chapters 2 and 3 evidence of 807 tombs from Shakhoura and Hamad Town was presented. A few of them (fourteen tombs) have been excluded from the sample due to lack of information, which is often caused by the fact that these tombs were not fully excavated. Twenty-five tombs were dated to the Dilmun period and have therefore also been excluded. The remaining 768 tombs are suitable for further discussion, of which 227 are from Hamad Town and 541 from Shakhoura. The above data will be supplemented with already published data to increase the sample size, especially regarding determinations of sex and age, which have not been carried out on the skeletal remains from Shakhoura. The dataset has, however, many limitations. Some of them relate to the methodology of the excavations and others to the burials themselves. The burial tradition of the Tylos period remained in use for a long time, perhaps for up to 900 years. Many tombs were reused for further interments, but probably the most significant factor is the relatively limited number of types of grave goods in each tomb, making analysis of combinations of categories of grave goods less rewarding.

The Tombs

Of the 768 tombs, 751 have the length of the tomb chamber recorded and if we look at this figure for the tomb in all periods in Hamad Town and Shakhoura it is evident that in both cemeteries the tombs can be divided into two groups. The great majority of tombs measure from 170 to 240 cm long and there is a smaller group of tombs that measures from 100 to 130 cm long.

[10] Interpretations of the social organization of ancient societies based on burials have been widely discussed. For recent reviews see e.g. Pearson 1999: 72–123, Jensen & Nielsen 1997.

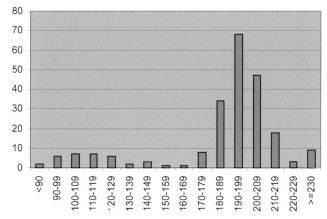

Figure 377. Length of tombs from Hamad Town.

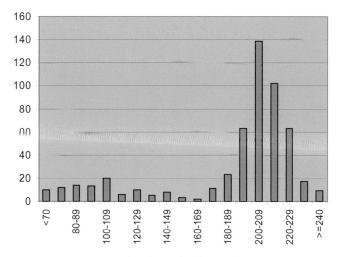

Figure 378. Length of tombs from Shakhoura.

Subadults (c. 2–15 years) were often buried in tombs smaller than those used for adults (Littleton 1998: 24). For 111 tombs from Hamad Town and from available reports from Saar, Karranah and al-Maqsha, we have both the length of the tomb chamber and an estimation of age based on skeletal remains from a single burial in the tomb. Ninety-five tombs were 170 cm or longer and only five of these contained a deceased less than c. 10 years old. Sixteen tombs were shorter than 170 cm and in fourteen of these the deceased was estimated to be less than c. 10 years old. Since the frequency of adults in tombs of 170 cm or longer is 95.8 % and the frequency of children in tombs of less than 170 cm is 87.5 %, it is reasonable to suggest that tombs of less than

170 cm were built for children. The reuse of tombs made for children seems to be very rare.

As regards the dating, only tombs containing one or more datable vessels can be included. If two vessels found together were assigned dates of two different phases, the discussions of the individual types and tomb assemblages in Volume 1 were consulted and only the most likely date for the tomb was used here, without repeating the chronological discussions.

	I	II	III	IV	
Shakhoura	9	39	104	1	153
Hamad Town	3	2	24	9	38
Total	12	41	128	10	191

Table 71. Number of datable tombs from Shakhoura and Hamad Town.

Only 191 of the 768 tombs can be dated and by far the majority of the dated tombs relates to Phase III (See Table 71).

Phase	Number	Length
I	2	188
II	2	191
III	21	206
IV	9	192

Table 72. Number of datable tombs (170 cm or above) and average length in Phases I to IV from Hamad Town.

Only thirty-four tombs of 170 cm or above can be dated in the Hamad Town cemetery and the majority date to Phase III. Although the numbers are small, it is interesting to observe that the tombs from Phase III are longer than the earlier and later ones. Since Phase III has been understood as a period of prosperity on Bahrain, this could indicate that the building of tombs reflects wealth to some degree, but nothing demonstrates social stratification.

Phase	Number	Ave. length
I	5	204,40
II	36	226,53
III	75	210,60
IV	1	225,00

Table 73. Number of datable tombs and average length in Phases I to IV from Shakhoura.

Looking at the similar figures from Shakhoura it can be observed that the tombs are longest in Phase II. In this phase, some of the tombs from Mound A1-1996-97 have a stepped frame, which adds some splendour to the tomb (see Chapter 3). This, together with the longer tombs, could indicate that more resources were spent building the tombs in Phase II in Shakhoura.

The tombs in Shakhoura are in all periods longer than those in Hamad Town, which supports the conclusions of a harder life in Hamad Town made from a comparative study of the skeletal remains from Hamad Town and Saar (Littleton 1998).[11] There seem therefore to be minor chronological and regional differences in the size of tombs, which may reflect the fact that slightly more resources were available in certain areas in certain periods. It has been argued that the increase in quantity of grave goods mainly in Phase III could relate to an increase in wealth. This could be due to benefits of the international trade between the Roman Empire and India, which probably started in Phase II. The people buried in Shakhoura may have benefited at this early stage and expressed their new position by building slightly larger tombs. This could be a result of Shakhoura being close to Qala'at al-Bahrain, which so far is the only known town of the period. In Phase III the prosperity spread to most parts of Bahrain and the tombs in Hamad Town became larger. However, again it must be emphasized that nothing indicates that different strata of society are expressed in the burials, since the differences are very small. Hereafter in Phase IV the trade routes or the organization of the trade may have changed, leaving only a minor profit in Bahrain (see Volume 1).

Many tombs also contained grave goods: in Hamad Town 49 % and in Shakhoura 44 %. Comparing the tomb length with the absence or presence of grave goods should show if the tombs and the grave goods indicate some social segmentation of society. In Hamad Town, the ninety-three tombs that did not contain grave goods had an average length of 198 cm whereas the ninety-one tombs with grave goods measured 199 cm on average. The similar figures for Shakhoura are 237 tombs/207 cm and 187 tombs/214 cm. Although there is a slight difference in Shakhoura between tombs with and tombs without grave goods, it is questionable if a 7 cm difference is noticeable in the appearance of the tomb. Furthermore, there is no significant relation between the amount of grave goods and the length, not even within one period (Phase III). Looking at the depth of the tombs and whether the tomb has been built into, on or above the bedrock, a similar coherent picture develops.

[11] Saar is geographically close to Shakhoura and the burials appear to be very similar to the ones in Shakhoura.

The layout of tombs within a mound, where relatively rich tombs are placed next to poorly equipped ones, without any notable difference in size and design of the tombs, supports the impression from the quantitative analysis of the tombs and grave goods presented above. All the evidence indicates a relatively egalitarian society where minor differences can be understood in a chronological and regional perspective and do not indicate social stratification. Of course, it cannot be excluded that the burials do not reflect status if there was a different segment of society which practised other burial traditions in Bahrain in the Tylos period, but we have no such evidence. The burial data indicate an egalitarian society, which in this way appears to be very different from the Bronze Age, where mounds of different categories were clearly constructed for different sectors of society, from very small mounds with simple tomb chambers to very large mounds with a complicated internal layout of burial chambers (see Højlund 2007).

Gender and age

Eighty-five tombs with a chamber length of 170 cm or above have an individual burial where the sex has been determined. Forty-five of these tombs contained a female and these tombs had an average length of 196 cm. The forty tombs containing a male had an average length of 197 cm. The sex, therefore, does not seem to influence the length of the tomb, an observation also noted by Littleton (1998: 24). For the choice of grave goods versus gender, the situation may be different. In the introduction, different categories of grave goods were briefly described and in the following, the relation between these categories and gender will be discussed.

A total of 103 tombs contained a single adult burial where the sex was determined.[12] Since skeletal remains were not always well preserved (Littleton 1998: 23–24), there may of course be a risk of "contamination" from undetected burials.

[12] For eighteen tombs with an individual burial where the sex was determined, there are no recordings of the length of the tomb, hence the difference between the figures.

Sex/gifts	Gifts	No gifts	Total
Female	38	20	58
Male	32	13	45
Total	70	33	103

Table 74. Number of tombs with or without gifts versus sex.

From Table 74 it can be observed that 66 % of the female tombs contained grave goods and 71 % of the male burials. This difference is minor and it can thus be assumed that gender did not affect the choice of whether or not to place grave goods in the tombs.

Of the 103 individual burials, fifty-eight are of females and forty-five of males. The difference in the number of males and females appears at first interesting, since Bahrain was a seafaring and fishing nation and probably with males manning the ships. The males are thus more likely to die far from their homes and cemeteries than the females, who most likely stayed behind. However, the difference is not significant in the light of the sample size, which is confirmed by checking the full inventory of skeletons where male and females are equally represented.

Seventy tombs contained an individual burial with gifts and had the sex of the deceased determined. Since no individual burials from Phase IV have been identified, these results probably apply only to Phases I–III.

Sex/Phase	I	II	III	Total
Female	5	7	7	19
Male	9	1	12	22
Total	14	8	19	41

Table 75. Number of datable tombs with grave goods, where sex has been determined.

Only forty-one of the seventy tombs can be dated (Table 75). The sample becomes too small if one attempts to analyse the content of different categories of grave goods within a chronological framework. However, if we assume that there are no significant differences between the various periods, it is possi-

Sex/categories	Food	Coin	Tableware	Misc.	Bead	Container	Jewellery	Shell	Pin
Female	2	3	25	3	10	10	8	6	16
Male	4	5	28	2	6	3	2	1	1
Total	6	8	53	5	16	13	10	7	17

Table 76. Number of tombs with certain categories of grave goods versus sex.

Sex/categories	Food	Coin	Tableware	Misc.	Bead	Container	Jewellery	Shell	Pin
Female	3%	5%	43%	5%	17%	17%	14%	10%	28%
Male	9%	11%	62%	4%	13%	7%	4%	2%	2%

Table 77. Frequency of tombs containing different categories of grave goods versus the sex of the deceased.

ble to see if there is any relation between categories of grave goods and gender, and the larger sample (seventy tombs) can thus be used.

Since more female burials have been recorded, the figures in Table 76 are not directly comparable, but by calculating the frequency of male and female tombs where the different categories are represented comparable figures can be obtained.

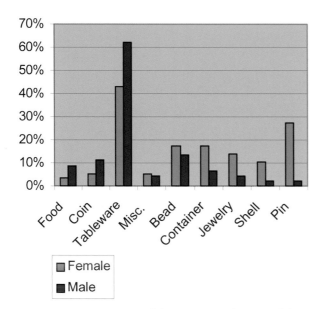

Figure 379. Diagram of frequencies from Table 77.

Thirty-four per cent of the female tombs and 29 % of the male tombs did not contain any detected grave goods. Tableware is the most common grave good for both sexes, since 62 % of the male tombs contained tableware and 43 % of the females were accompanied by tableware. The tableware vessels are likely to have had a representative value as symbols of or as actual containers for provision for the journey to the afterworld. From Phase I to Phase III cups or small bowls are often found upside down on the capstone of the tomb and filled with ash (Jensen 2003: 133; al-Sindi & Salman 1999: 159). In some instances remnants of food have been found, most often chicken bones and eggshells, and also a date stone and some lamb bones. These finds could well

represent unique choices, since bread, milk products or gruel may have played a more prominent role in the diet, but they would not have been detected with the methodology applied in the excavations. Food documented directly or indirectly by the presence of tableware seems therefore to have played an important role in the funeral ceremonies and may at least in Phases I to III have been a necessity to ensure a safe journey to the afterworld.

Most categories can be found with both males and females. Fragments of kohl-sticks, spatulas, dress pins, distaffs and spindles (pin category) are associated with females, since only one fragment has been found with a skeleton identified as male. In nearly a third of the female burials one or more fragments of pins have been found. This could be a matter of preservation, since most bone and metal from the tombs is much deteriorated and it is thus likely that more tombs have contained pins. The use of spindles and distaffs as female symbols in funeral contexts is well known in Palmyra in the first centuries AD where they are commonly depicted with females on funeral reliefs. It has been suggested that they were symbols of the housewife, but the spindles and distaffs are also found on reliefs attributed to unmarried females, which indicates that the symbolic meaning may only relate to the sex of the deceased (Hvidberg-Hansen & Ploug 1993: 44). A similar function can well be applied to the Bahraini assemblages. The shells and perfume containers are also over-represented in feminine burials and the single shell found accompanying a male could well be a coincidence. These two groups may however have had other functions, as indicated by the glass date flask found with a large collection of tools (e.g. a knife, awl, needle and other tools) in Saar (Herling 2003: 492–494, abb. 150). Such a large collection of tools is very rare in the tombs and it is therefore possible that the glass flask in this specific tomb is a result of a unique handicraft association, distinct from its standard function as an unguent container. The two remaining containers found with males may also have been chosen for special reasons, since one was found with a bone plaque (Karranah, Mound 1-1993, Tomb C III 3) and the other with a ring of unknown material (Hamad Town, Mound 71-85-86, Tomb 9). It is therefore likely that containers and seashells were

Appendix 1

List of finds from Saar, Mound 5-87-88 recorded in the storeroom at Bahrain National Museum. The datings are derived from Volume 1.

Context	Number	Material	Type	Number	Phase
Jar		Glass & stone	Bead	13	
Jar	8	Glass & stone	Bead	N/A	I
Jar	8	Glazed ware	Bowl	1	I
Jar	9	Glass & stone	Bead	121	
Jar	25	Glass	Bead	12	
Mound Fill		Glass & stone	Bead	2	
Mound Fill		Glass & stone	Bead	N/A	
Tomb	1	Glass & stone	Bead	3	III
Tomb	1	Glazed ware	Bottle	1	III
Tomb	2	Gold	Bead	2	III
Tomb	2	Glass	Plate	1	III
Tomb	2	Lead	Pendant	1	III
Tomb	3	Stone	Bead	2	
Tomb	5	Glazed ware	Cup	1	
Tomb	6	Glazed ware	Bowl	1	II
Tomb	7	Glazed ware	Bottle	1	II
Tomb	7	Glazed ware	Bowl	1	II
Tomb	7	Bronze	Coin	1	II
Tomb	10	Glass & stone	Bead	3	
Tomb	11	Glazed ware	Bowl	1	III
Tomb	11	Glazed ware	Crater	1	III
Tomb	13	Glazed ware	Bowl	1	II
Tomb	13	Grey ware	Bowl	1	II
Tomb	14	Glazed ware	Plate	1	
Tomb	15	Bronze	Spatula	0	III
Tomb	15	Glazed ware	Bowl	1	III
Tomb	15	Glass & stone	Bead	N/A	III
Tomb	19	Glass	Cup	1	IV
Tomb	20	Glass & stone	Bead	12	
Tomb	22	Silver	Coin	1	II
Tomb	22	Stone	Gem	1	II
Tomb	22	Glazed ware	Bottle	1	II
Tomb	22	Glazed ware	Bowl	1	II
Tomb	22	Glass & stone	Bead	N/A	II
Tomb	22	Silver	Finger ring	1	II
Tomb	22	Ivory	Pin	1	II
Tomb	23	Sand-tempered ware	Bowl	1	
Tomb	24	Glazed ware	Bowl	1	II
Tomb	24	Glazed ware	Cup	1	II
Tomb	25	Glazed ware	Cup	1	III
Tomb	25	Stone	Bead	9	III
Tomb	25	Glass & stone	Bead	N/A	III
Tomb	25	Glazed ware	Bottle	1	III

Tomb	27	Hard-fired ware	Jug	1	III
Tomb	27	Glazed ware	Bottle	1	III
Tomb	27	Bronze	Bell	1	III
Tomb	28	Glazed ware	Cup	1	II
Tomb	29	Glazed ware	Cup	1	III
Tomb	29	Glass & stone	Bead	N/A	III
Tomb	31	Grey ware	Bowl	1	I
Tomb	31	Grey ware	Bowl	1	I
Tomb	32	Glass & stone	Bead	13	III
Tomb	32	Glazed ware	Bowl	1	III
Tomb	34	Glazed ware	Bowl	1	II
Tomb	35	Bronze	Pin	1	III
Tomb	35	Glazed ware	Bottle	1	III
Tomb	35	Glazed ware	Cup	1	III
Tomb	35	Ivory	Pin head	6	III
Tomb	35	Glass & stone	Bead	N/A	III
Tomb	36	Glazed ware	Jug	1	II
Tomb	39	Glazed ware	Cup	1	III
Tomb	40	Glass & stone	Bead	N/A	III
Tomb	40	Glazed ware	Bowl	1	III
Tomb	40	Bronze	Bell	3	III
Tomb	41	Glazed ware	Cup	1	III
Tomb	42	Glazed ware	Cup	1	II
Tomb	42	Glazed ware	Bowl	1	II
Tomb	43	Glazed ware	Cup	1	II
Tomb	44	Glazed ware	Cup	1	III
Tomb	45	Glass & stone	Bead	14	
Tomb	45	Pottery	Weight	2	
Tomb	46	Glazed ware	Cup	1	
Tomb	46	Glass & stone	Bead	N/A	
Tomb	47	Stone	Bead	3	
Tomb	49	Glass	Bottle	1	IV
Tomb	49	Glass	Bottle	1	IV
Tomb	49	Glass	Bottle	1	IV
Tomb	49	Glass	Bottle	1	IV
Tomb	49	Glass	Bottle	1	IV
Tomb	49	Glass	Bottle	1	IV
Tomb	49	Glass	Bottle	1	IV
Tomb	49	Glass & stone	Bead	N/A	IV
Tomb	51	Stone	N/A	7	II
Tomb	51	Seashell	N/A	4	II
Tomb	51	Glazed ware	Bowl	1	II
Tomb	51	Glazed ware	Bowl	1	II
Tomb	51	Glass & stone	Bead	N/A	II
Tomb	53	Bronze	Finger ring	2	
Tomb	55	Glazed ware	Crater	1	II
Tomb	56	Glazed ware	Cup	1	
Tomb	56	Glazed ware	Bowl	1	
Tomb	58	Plain ware	Bowl	1	
Tomb	59	Glazed ware	Bowl	1	III

Tomb	63	Glazed ware	Bowl	2	III
Tomb	66	Glazed ware	Cup	1	II
Tomb	69	Glass	Cup	1	IV
Tomb	70	Glazed ware	Cup	1	III
Tomb	71	Glass & stone	Bead	3	
Tomb	72	Glass & stone	Bead	N/A	
Tomb	77	Red ware	Bowl	1	I
Tomb	78	Glazed ware	Crater	1	II
Tomb	81	Glass & stone	Bead	N/A	
Tomb	83	Glazed ware	Cup	1	III
Tomb	83	Glazed ware	Crater	1	III
Tomb	83	Glazed ware	Bowl	1	III
Tomb	94	Glazed ware	Bowl	1	III
Tomb	94	Glass	Bottle	1	III
Tomb	96	Glass & stone	Bead	N/A	
Tomb	101	Bronze	Coin?	1	
Tomb	101	Bronze	Bell	1	
Tomb	101	Glass & stone	Bead	18	

Appendix 2

Judith Littleton

List of determination of sex and age from the skeletal remains.

Area	Mound	Season	Context	Number	Skeleton	Sex	Age	Phase
Hamad Town DS3	30	1985-86	Jar	1	Single	N/A	Infant	
Hamad Town DS3	30	1985-86	Jar	2	Single	N/A	Infant	
Hamad Town DS3	30	1985-86	Jar	4	Single	N/A	Infant	
Hamad Town DS3	30	1985-86	Jar	6	Single	N/A	Infant	
Hamad Town DS3	30	1985-86	Tomb	1	Single	Male	Adult	
Hamad Town DS3	30	1985-86	Tomb	12	Multi			
Hamad Town DS3	30	1985-86	Tomb	13	Multi			
Hamad Town DS3	30	1985-86	Tomb	14	Multi			
Hamad Town DS3	30	1985-86	Tomb	15	Single	Female	Adult	
Hamad Town DS3	30	1985-86	Tomb	16	Multi			
Hamad Town DS3	30	1985-86	Tomb	17	Single	N/A	Infant	
Hamad Town DS3	30	1985-86	Tomb	18	Single	N/A	Infant	
Hamad Town DS3	30	1985-86	Tomb	19	Single	Male	Adult	
Hamad Town DS3	30	1985-86	Tomb	2	Multi			
Hamad Town DS3	30	1985-86	Tomb	20	Single	Female	Adult	
Hamad Town DS3	30	1985-86	Tomb	21	Single	Female	Adult	II
Hamad Town DS3	30	1985-86	Tomb	22	Single	Female	Adult	
Hamad Town DS3	30	1985-86	Tomb	25	Single	Female	Adult	
Hamad Town DS3	30	1985-86	Tomb	27	Single	Female	Adult	
Hamad Town DS3	30	1985-86	Tomb	28	Multi			
Hamad Town DS3	30	1985-86	Tomb	3	Single	Female	Adult	
Hamad Town DS3	30	1985-86	Tomb	33	Multi			II
Hamad Town DS3	30	1985-86	Tomb	34	Multi			
Hamad Town DS3	30	1985-86	Tomb	38	Multi			
Hamad Town DS3	30	1985-86	Tomb	39	Single	Female	Adult	
Hamad Town DS3	30	1985-86	Tomb	4	Single	Female	Adult	
Hamad Town DS3	30	1985-86	Tomb	40	Multi			III
Hamad Town DS3	30	1985-86	Tomb	41	Single	Male	Adult	III
Hamad Town DS3	30	1985-86	Tomb	5	Multi			
Hamad Town DS3	30	1985-86	Tomb	6	Multi			
Hamad Town DS3	30	1985-86	Tomb	8	Multi			
Hamad Town DS3	70A	1985-86	Tomb	1	Multi			III
Hamad Town DS3	70A	1985-86	Tomb	10	Multi			
Hamad Town DS3	70A	1985-86	Tomb	11	Multi			
Hamad Town DS3	70A	1985-86	Tomb	13	Single	Female	Adult	
Hamad Town DS3	70A	1985-86	Tomb	18	Single	Female	Adult	
Hamad Town DS3	70A	1985-86	Tomb	19	Single	Female	Adult	
Hamad Town DS3	70A	1985-86	Tomb	2	Multi			
Hamad Town DS3	70A	1985-86	Tomb	5	Multi			
Hamad Town DS3	70A	1985-86	Tomb	6	Multi			IV
Hamad Town DS3	70A	1985-86	Tomb	7	Single	N/A	Subadult	
Hamad Town DS3	70A	1985-86	Tomb	9	Multi			
Hamad Town DS3	71	1985-86	Tomb	1	Single	Male	Adult	
Hamad Town DS3	71	1985-86	Tomb	10	Multi			
Hamad Town DS3	71	1985-86	Tomb	11	Single	Male	Adult	
Hamad Town DS3	71	1985-86	Tomb	13	Single	Male	Adult	

Hamad Town DS3	71	1985-86	Tomb	15	Single	N/A	Subadult	
Hamad Town DS3	71	1985-86	Tomb	5	Single	Male	Adult	
Hamad Town DS3	71	1985-86	Tomb	6	Single	Female	Subadult	
Hamad Town DS3	71	1985-86	Tomb	7	Multi			
Hamad Town DS3	71	1985-86	Tomb	9	Single	Male	Adult	
Hamad Town DS3	73	1985-86	Jar	6	Multi			
Hamad Town DS3	73	1985-86	Tomb	1	Multi			IV
Hamad Town DS3	73	1985-86	Tomb	10	Single	Male	Adult	
Hamad Town DS3	73	1985-86	Tomb	11	Multi			
Hamad Town DS3	73	1985-86	Tomb	13	Single	Female	Adult	
Hamad Town DS3	73	1985-86	Tomb	14	Multi			
Hamad Town DS3	73	1985-86	Tomb	15	Single	Female	Adult	
Hamad Town DS3	73	1985-86	Tomb	16	Single	Female	Adult	
Hamad Town DS3	73	1985-86	Tomb	17	Single	N/A	Subadult	
Hamad Town DS3	73	1985-86	Tomb	18A	Multi			
Hamad Town DS3	73	1985-86	Tomb	18B	Multi			
Hamad Town DS3	73	1985-86	Tomb	18C	Multi			
Hamad Town DS3	73	1985-86	Tomb	18D	Multi			
Hamad Town DS3	73	1985-86	Tomb	18E	Multi			
Hamad Town DS3	73	1985-86	Tomb	19	Single	Female	Adult	III
Hamad Town DS3	73	1985-86	Tomb	2	Single	Female	Adult	
Hamad Town DS3	73	1985-86	Tomb	20	Multi			
Hamad Town DS3	73	1985-86	Tomb	21	Single	Female	Adult	
Hamad Town DS3	73	1985-86	Tomb	22	Multi			
Hamad Town DS3	73	1985-86	Tomb	23	Single	Female	Adult	
Hamad Town DS3	73	1985-86	Tomb	25	Multi			
Hamad Town DS3	73	1985-86	Tomb	26	Multi			
Hamad Town DS3	73	1985-86	Tomb	27	Single	N/A	Subadult	III
Hamad Town DS3	73	1985-86	Tomb	28	Single	Female	Adult	III
Hamad Town DS3	73	1985-86	Tomb	29	Multi			
Hamad Town DS3	73	1985-86	Tomb	3	Multi			
Hamad Town DS3	73	1985-86	Tomb	33	Multi			III
Hamad Town DS3	73	1985-86	Tomb	34	Single	Female	Adult	III
Hamad Town DS3	73	1985-86	Tomb	35	Single	Female	Adult	
Hamad Town DS3	73	1985-86	Tomb	36	Single	Male	Adult	III
Hamad Town DS3	73	1985-86	Tomb	37	Single	Female	Adult	III
Hamad Town DS3	73	1985-86	Tomb	39	Single	Female	Adult	
Hamad Town DS3	73	1985-86	Tomb	4	Single	Male	Adult	III
Hamad Town DS3	73	1985-86	Tomb	40	Single	Female	Adult	
Hamad Town DS3	73	1985-86	Tomb	41	Multi			III
Hamad Town DS3	73	1985-86	Tomb	42	Single	Female	Adult	
Hamad Town DS3	73	1985-86	Tomb	43	Single	N/A	Subadult	
Hamad Town DS3	73	1985-86	Tomb	44	Multi			IV
Hamad Town DS3	73	1985-86	Tomb	45	Multi			
Hamad Town DS3	73	1985-86	Tomb	46	Single	N/A	Subadult	
Hamad Town DS3	73	1985-86	Tomb	48	Single	Female	Adult	
Hamad Town DS3	73	1985-86	Tomb	5	Multi			
Hamad Town DS3	73	1985-86	Tomb	50	Single	Male	Adult	
Hamad Town DS3	73	1985-86	Tomb	51	Multi			III
Hamad Town DS3	73	1985-86	Tomb	52	Single	Male	Adult	III
Hamad Town DS3	73	1985-86	Tomb	53	Single	N/A	Subadult	III
Hamad Town DS3	73	1985-86	Tomb	54	Multi			III
Hamad Town DS3	73	1985-86	Tomb	55	Single	Female	Adult	III

Hamad Town DS3	73	1985-86	Tomb	57	Single	Female	Adult	
Hamad Town DS3	73	1985-86	Tomb	61	Single	Female	Adult	
Hamad Town DS3	73	1985-86	Tomb	62	Single	N/A	Subadult	
Hamad Town DS3	73	1985-86	Tomb	65	Single	Female	Adult	
Hamad Town DS3	73	1985-86	Tomb	7	Multi			
Hamad Town DS3	73	1985-86	Tomb	8	Single	N/A	Subadult	III
Hamad Town DS3	73	1985-86	Tomb	9	Multi			
Hamad Town DS3	81	1985-86	Tomb	1	Single	Male	Adult	
Hamad Town DS3	81	1985-86	Tomb	10	Single	Male	Adult	
Hamad Town DS3	81	1985-86	Tomb	11	Single	Male	Adult	III
Hamad Town DS3	81	1985-86	Tomb	12	Multi			
Hamad Town DS3	81	1985-86	Tomb	13	Multi			
Hamad Town DS3	81	1985-86	Tomb	15	Multi			
Hamad Town DS3	81	1985-86	Tomb	4	Single	Male	Adult	
Hamad Town DS3	81	1985-86	Tomb	5	Single	Male	Adult	
Hamad Town DS3	81	1985-86	Tomb	7	Single	N/A	Subadult	
Hamad Town DS3	81	1985-86	Tomb	9	Multi			
Hamad Town DS3	83	1985-86	Jar	10	Single	N/A	Infant	
Hamad Town DS3	83	1985-86	Jar	4	Single	N/A	Subadult	
Hamad Town DS3	83	1985-86	Jar	7	Single	N/A	Infant	
Hamad Town DS3	83	1985-86	Jar	8	Single	N/A	Infant	III
Hamad Town DS3	83	1985-86	Jar	9	Single	N/A	Infant	
Hamad Town DS3	83	1985-86	Tomb	1	Multi			
Hamad Town DS3	83	1985-86	Tomb	11	Single	N/A	Subadult	
Hamad Town DS3	83	1985-86	Tomb	12	Single	Female	Adult	
Hamad Town DS3	83	1985-86	Tomb	13	Single	Female	Adult	
Hamad Town DS3	83	1985-86	Tomb	14	Single	Female	Adult	
Hamad Town DS3	83	1985-86	Tomb	15	Multi			
Hamad Town DS3	83	1985-86	Tomb	16	Multi			
Hamad Town DS3	83	1985-86	Tomb	17	Single	Male	Adult	
Hamad Town DS3	83	1985-86	Tomb	18	Multi			
Hamad Town DS3	83	1985-86	Tomb	2	Multi			
Hamad Town DS3	83	1985-86	Tomb	20	Multi			
Hamad Town DS3	83	1985-86	Tomb	22	Multi			
Hamad Town DS3	83	1985-86	Tomb	23	Single			
Hamad Town DS3	83	1985-86	Tomb	24	Multi			
Hamad Town DS3	83	1985-86	Tomb	26	Multi			IV
Hamad Town DS3	83	1985-86	Tomb	28	Multi			
Hamad Town DS3	83	1985-86	Tomb	28	Multi			
Hamad Town DS3	83	1985-86	Tomb	29	Multi			
Hamad Town DS3	83	1985 86	Tomb	29	Single			
Hamad Town DS3	83	1985-86	Tomb	3	Multi			
Hamad Town DS3	83	1985-86	Tomb	30	Multi			
Hamad Town DS3	83	1985-86	Tomb	31	Multi			IV
Hamad Town DS3	83	1985-86	Tomb	32	Multi			
Hamad Town DS3	83	1985-86	Tomb	33	Single	N/A	Infant	
Hamad Town DS3	83	1985-86	Tomb	34	Single	Male	Adult	
Hamad Town DS3	83	1985-86	Tomb	35	Single	Female	Adult	
Hamad Town DS3	83	1985-86	Tomb	36	Single	Male	Adult	
Hamad Town DS3	83	1985-86	Tomb	37	Single	Male	Adult	
Hamad Town DS3	83	1985-86	Tomb	38	Single	N/A	Adult	
Hamad Town DS3	83	1985-86	Tomb	40	Single	N/A	Subadult	
Hamad Town DS3	83	1985-86	Tomb	42	Multi			III

Hamad Town DS3	83	1985-86	Tomb	43	Single	N/A	Infant	III
Hamad Town DS3	83	1985-86	Tomb	44	Multi			IV
Hamad Town DS3	83	1985-86	Tomb	45	Multi			
Hamad Town DS3	83	1985-86	Tomb	47	Multi			
Hamad Town DS3	83	1985-86	Tomb	49	Single	N/A	Infant	
Hamad Town DS3	83	1985-86	Tomb	5	Multi			
Hamad Town DS3	83	1985-86	Tomb	52	Single	N/A	Infant	
Hamad Town DS3	83	1985-86	Tomb	6	Multi			
Hamad Town DS3	83	1985-86	Tomb	7	Multi			
Hamad Town DS3	83	1985-86	Tomb	8	Single	Female	Adult	
Hamad Town DS3	83	1985-86	Tomb	9	Single	Male	Adult	
Hamad Town DS3	88	85-86	Tomb	2	Multi			
Hamad Town DS3	88	85-86	Tomb	3	Multi			
Hamad Town DS3	88	85-86	Tomb	4	Multi			
Saar	5	1987-88	Tomb	2	Multi			III
Saar	5	1987-88	Tomb	3	Multi			
Saar	5	1987-88	Tomb	5	Single	N/A	Adult	
Saar	5	1987-88	Tomb	7	Single	Female	Adult	II
Saar	5	1987-88	Tomb	10	Single	N/A	Infant	
Saar	5	1987-88	Tomb	11	Multi			III
Saar	5	1987-88	Tomb	13	Multi			II
Saar	5	1987-88	Tomb	19	Single	N/A	Infant	IV
Saar	5	1987-88	Tomb	24	Single	Female	Adult	II
Saar	5	1987-88	Tomb	25	Single	Female	Adult	III
Saar	5	1987-88	Tomb	31	Single	Female	Adult	I
Saar	5	1987-88	Tomb	32	Single	N/A	Infant	III
Saar	5	1987-88	Tomb	34	Single	Female	Adult	II
Saar	5	1987-88	Tomb	35	Single	Female	Adult	III
Saar	5	1987-88	Tomb	40	Multi			III
Saar	5	1987-88	Tomb	41	Single	N/A	Subadult	III
Saar	5	1987-88	Tomb	46	Single	Male	Adult	
Saar	5	1987-88	Tomb	47	Single	N/A	Subadult	
Saar	5	1987-88	Tomb	49	Multi			IV
Saar	5	1987-88	Tomb	51	Single	N/A	Subadult	II
Saar	5	1987-88	Tomb	53	Single	Female	Adult	
Saar	5	1987-88	Tomb	55	Single	Female	Adult	II
Saar	5	1987-88	Tomb	56	Multi			
Saar	5	1987-88	Tomb	58	Single	Female	Adult	
Saar	5	1987-88	Tomb	63	Single	N/A	Subadult	III
Saar	5	1987-88	Tomb	66	Multi			II
Saar	5	1987-88	Tomb	69	Multi			IV
Saar	5	1987-88	Tomb	72	Multi			
Saar	5	1987-88	Tomb	77	Multi			I
Saar	5	1987-88	Tomb	78	Multi			II
Saar	5	1987-88	Tomb	83	Single	Male	Adult	III

Bibliography

Andersen, S.F. (2007)
The Tylos period Burials on Bahrain. Vol.
1. *The Glass Vessels and Tableware Pottery*.
Manama.

Andersen, S.F., Salman M.I., Strehle, H. & Tengberg, M. (2004)
Two wooden coffins from the Shakhoura Necropolis, Bahrain. *Arabian Archaeology and Epigraphy* 15/2: 219–228.

Bibby, T.G. (1954)
Fem af Bahrains hundrede tusinde gravhøje.
Kuml 1954: 116–141.

Campbell, S. & Green, A. (eds) (1995)
The Archaeology of Death in the Ancient Near East. Oxbow Monograph, 51. Exeter.

Curtis, J.E. (1995)
Gold face-masks in the ancient Near East. Pages 227-231 in Campbell & Green 1995.

Dentzer-Feydy, J. & Teixidor, J. (1993)
Les antiquités de Palmyre au Musée du Louvre. Paris.

Field, H. (1951)
Reconnaissance in Southwestern Asia. *Southwestern Journal of Anthropology* 7/1: 86–102.
Albuquerque, NM.

Gatier, P-L., Lombard, P. & al-Sindi, K. (2002)
Greek Inscriptions from Bahrain. *Arabian Archaeology and Epigraphy* 13/2: 223–233.

Haerinck, E. (2001)
Excavations at ed-Dur (Umm al-Qaiwain, United Arab Emirates)/the University of Ghent South-East Arabian archaeological project. Vol. 2. *The tombs*. Leuven.

Herling, A. (1999)
Nécropoles et coutumes funéraires à l'époque de Tylos. Pages 150–155 in Lombard 1999.

——————— (2003)
Tyloszeitliche Bestattungspraktiken auf der Insel Bahrain. Bd 1–3. Göttingen.

Herling, A., Latzel, M., Littleton, J., Möllering, I., Schippmann, K. & Velde, C. (1993)
Excavation at Karranah Mound I (1992). [Unpublished report].

Højlund, F. (2007)
The Burial Mounds of Bahrain. Social complexity in Early Dilmun. Højbjerg.

Højlund, F. & Andersen, H.H. (1994)
Qala'at al-Bahrain. Vol. 1. Jutland Archaeological Society Publications, 30/1. Aarhus.

Hvidberg-Hansen, F.O. & Ploug, G. (1993)
Katalog Palmyra samlingen, Ny Carlsberg Glyptotek. Copenhagen.

Ivanova, A.P., Cubova, A.P. & Kolesnikova, L.G. (1976)
Antichnaja skulptura Chersonesa. Kiev.

Jensen, S.T. (2003)
Tylos burials from three different sites on Bahrain. *Arabian Archaeology and Epigraphy* 14/2: 127–163.

Jensen, C.K & Nielsen, K.H. (eds) (1997)
Burial & Society, The Chronological and Social Analysis of Archaeological Burial Data.
Aarhus.

Kennet, D. (2005)
On the eve of Islam: archaeological evidence from Eastern Arabia. *Antiquity* 79/303: 107-118.

Kolesnikova, L.G. (1977)
Znacenie i mesto antropomorphnych nadgrobij v nekropole Chersonesa. *Sovetskaja archeologija* 2: 87–99.

Littleton, J. (1998)
Skeletons and Social Composition, Bahrain 300 BC–AD 250. British Archaeological Reports, International Series, 703. Oxford.

Lombard, P. (ed) (1999)
Bahreïn, La civilisation des deux mers, de Dilmoun à Tylos. Ghent.

Lombard, P. & Salles J-F. (1984)
La Nécropole de Janussan. Travaux de la maison de l'Orient, no. 6. Lyon.

MacDonald, K.C. (2003)
The Domestic chicken in the Tylos burials of Bahrain. *Arabian Archaeology and Epigraphy* 14/2: 194–195.

Moscati, S. (2001)
The Phoenicians. London & New York.

Pearson, M.P. (1999)
The Archaeology of Death and Burial. Sparkford.

Penglase, C. (1995)
Some Concepts of Afterlife in Mesopotamia and Greece. Pages 192–195 in Campbell & Green 1995.

Sader, H. (2005)
Iron Age Funerary Stelae from Lebanon. Cuadernos de Arqueología Mediteránea, 11. El Prat de Llobregat.

Simpson, StJ. (1995)
Death and burial in the Late Islamic Near East: Some Insights from Archaeology and Ethnography. Pages 240–251 in Campbell & Green 1995.

Simpson, StJ. (ed.) (2002)
Queen of Sheba, Treasures from Ancient Yemen. Barcelona.

al-Sindi, K. & Salman, M.I. (1999)
Une nécropole représentative des diverses phases de Tylos: le Mont I de Shakhoura. Pages 156–159 in Lombard 1999.

Vogt, B. (2002)
Dead and Funerary Practices. Pages 180–207 in Simpson 2002.

Yule, P. (2001)
Die Gräberfelder in Samad al Shãn (Sultanat Oman) — Materialien zu einer Kulturgeschichte-Text & Tafeln. Orient-Archäologie, Band 4. Rahden/Westf.